START YOUR OWN HIGH PROFIT THRIFT STORE

DON RUEHS

ISBN 10: 1-933817-52-6
ISBN 13: 978-1-933817-52-1

Published in the USA by
Profits Publishing of Sarasota, Florida
http://profitspublishing.com

Text Layout and Cover Design by
Marian of Profits Publishing

DISCLAIMER

Note: This book discusses common business, legal and accounting practices. However, the information is general in nature, and no legal, tax, or financial advice is given. If legal or other expert assistance is required, you should obtain the services of competent professionals.

Laws frequently change and vary from one location to another. Every effort is made to keep this book as current as possible. However, the author, the publisher, and the vendor of this book cannot make any representation or warranties regarding the outcome or the use to which the information in this book is put and are not assuming any liability for any claims, losses, or damages arising out of the use of this book. The reader must rely on professional advice and instruction, not the author or the publisher of this book for any professional advice.

ACKNOWLEDGEMENTS

Special thanks to Lyle for his constant support, encouragement and wonderful listening skills.

Lots of appreciation to Bob Burnham for his sage advice and motivational talks.

Garth has given generously of his time and numerous skills to prepare the photos and ads, for which I'm most grateful.

Table of Contents

About the Author

Donald Ruehs is an energetic, optimistic entrepreneur who in 25 years of successfully operating service oriented businesses has turned an initial loan of $5,000 into a cash capital of over one million dollars. His practical experience in managing a business, with all its challenges and opportunities is a strong contribution for his consulting and writing business.

His expertise in the recycling, and retail fields has resulted in his authoritative and valuable advice contained in this book. The key secrets of this business have been tested and are proven winners that you won't find anywhere else.

Author's Note:

This book is the perfect opportunity for:

- an enterprising entrepreneur,
- a resourceful fund raiser,
- serious environmentalist or
- a charitable organization

Whether used by an enterprising entrepreneur, a resourceful fund raiser, serious environmentalist or a charitable organization - these are simple, time proven formulas for success. This sort of business is definitely a way of the future and everything you need to set up and run a profitable, society conscious business is in this book.

From my 25 years experience as an entrepreneur I am glad to help others become successful.

I share with you, my practical experience, lessons learned along the way, and my training in business practices, This book will give you everything needed to start and run a successful business. I sincerely wish you every benefit and happiness. You can always contact me at www.startthriftstore.com.

Fear melts when you take action
towards a goal you really want.

Robert G Allen
Business, Finance & Motivational Author

Introduction:

Reasons Why You Will Benefit From Starting Your Own Thrift Store

You Will Make a Six Figure Income

There are enormous reasons why you will earn big bucks by selling used items. The future is so bright in this business that you have to wear shades.

First advantage is that you do not have to spend a single cent for your products.

Come to think of it, managing a business with very minimal capital, isn't that fantastic?

Just look around you and you'll be amazed of the many things you could actually make money out of. People all have old clothes, furniture, jewelry, books or what-have-you; all of these can be sold in no time.

Another plus is that recycling is now encouraged everywhere. It has rapidly developed into a trend.

People from all walks of life are thinking "green". Instead of buying new items, they would opt to grab the gently used ones as it promotes recycling. Some folks are into vintage stuff. They have a special yearning for things old & are willing to spend a fortune if something caught their fancies.

Most essentially, this kind of business will benefit the budget-conscious in all of us. One way or another, each one of us thinks of means to save money and are all concerned with our budgets. And that is where your thrift store comes in. Avid bargain hunters will certainly buy items they need & want so as to save them a penny or two.

As they say, "someone's trash is another's treasure".So what are you waiting for? Turn garbage scouting into treasure hunting!

You Do The Planet A Favor By Selling Used Goods

Our planet is in an energy crisis that will not solve itself.

Consumer goods & appliances require energy & resources in their creation, operation and disposal. This causes introduction of greenhouse gases, heavy metals & toxic chemicals that may harm the environment. However, you can help minimize this hazardous effect by gathering used items in your store and sell them at reasonable prices. You may have a habit of throwing things unwanted into the garbage bin, why not start segregating this stuff & become more planet-friendly? This will lessen the consuming of more energy by replacing or producing a new one & therefore doing our earth a favor.

You Really Can Do It !

If you are a bit hesitant, you can recall having had a garage sale. Afterwards, you will realize the fulfillment it brings having helped the earth in your little way. Stepping forward is the next best thing to do & that is running your own thrift store. Putting up one provides a greater opportunity to save energy & higher achievement to rescue our planet.

Do not wait for mother earth to grow tired of us. She gets weary producing too and people not making the most out of those products. Well, good news is that it is not too late yet and your efforts would not be put to waste if you start your own Thrift Store.

The future is in your hands. Save used items, sell them & save the earth. Simple yet a noble act.

You Will Be Your Own Boss

Are you tired of working so hard in a company with scanty compensation and very plain benefits? Do you think you can do a better job than your supervisor & can't wait to take his/her position?

If your answers are both "Yes" to these questions then I suggest you don't need to take your boss' place.

You can be your own boss if you let yourself become one.

The easiest way is to venture into managing a thrift shop. You are the law, you set your own rules and you can take a break anytime you please without asking someone else's permission.

LEARN VALUABLE SKILLS AS YOU MAKE MONEY

You take charge of the thrift store, all the ins & outs of the business. You will have a working team of your own but you are the sole leader who oversees everyone's tasks. Also, putting up a thrift store enhances your management skills as you experience daily responsibilities you may not have known if you did not venture into it.

Being a boss in a thrift storeyields a sense of fulfillmentnot found in other enterprises.

Gradually, you will learn and acquire a tremendous amount of valuable experiences and knowledge from the operation of your own business, just like I did.

You will be an unconventional manager who took "the road less traveled" and proud of it! An entrepreneur may opt for a food business but everyone's into it. It is a tough competition to get by. It is rather easy to become a boss in a thrift store where there is less competition yet huge opportunity.

You Will Become A Community Leader

Leaders are not born but we all have the ability to become one. You just need to have the urge to explore & break new ground. Begin with your community and you'll conquer the world without you even noticing it.

A great example of showing your leadership skill is having your own thrift store. With this in thought, you help build your community/neighborhood together.

People will look up to you not only as a community leader but also as a worthy role model.

Become Who You Really Are!

How can you be one? It is not a big task. You can initiate a simple get together with your community & encourage them to clear their respective houses to find some good quality used items to be sold. You can hold a mini-garage sale as a start. Later on, you can move forward to putting up your own thrift store. By this time you certainly have discovered more resources for your merchandise.

Charitable organizations are always looking to raise funds – at least one of them will be lucky enough to lend their name to your thrift store.

Your neighbors may even start their own thrift store business out of envy, but there is such a demand for bargains, it will generate more sales for you as the awareness increases. You are the pioneer in your community and you lead them to become more resourceful & creative of what they already have. You have given them an opportunity to explore their potentials. That is truly an uplifting feeling! You instantly became the legend, model & leader.

Being a leader does not have to be such a big deal after all as long as you have the enthusiasm to become one. It does not require dominating people, only a desire to differentiate yourself, to make your mark.

You Will Support Your Favorite Charity

Celebrities hold shows and or concerts to support their favorite charities. But for an average person like you & me, we obviously are not likely to do anything close to that.

The need for increased aid to helping charities has never been greater!

Whether it is for protection or rescue of animals or helping associations that spearhead research into illness.

Support for people with disabilities or children's sports league – they are all hungry and will flood your thrift store with lightly used goods that will sell quickly.

The good news is that you can maximize your resources by selling your second hand goods & allot some proceeds of it to go to your preferred institution/social welfare organizations.

Now, More Than Ever

It is brilliant - you can actually hit two birds with one stone. You earn a great share of income for your own needs & you also aid the less fortunate by putting up a thrift store.

And when you sell your slightly used items, you have already helped the charity because you unburden them of any time & money they would have spent on selling those goods. That is why charities these days tend to choose cash donations instead of goods since it allows them greater flexibility in spending the money so that it reaches the people that need it the most.

One does not have to be rich & famous to be able to give assistance to the needy. You can be ordinary yet as notable as your celebrity idol by simply managing your own thrift shop!

You Quickly Attract Loyal Customers

In this kind of business, it's very easy to attract loyal customers especially if you have good bargains and you give them a great customer experience each time they are around.

What's nice about having a thrift shop is that you'll get to mingle with different kinds of people. It's so overwhelming to see them very exuberant about something they found unique from your selections of used goods. There are even some who are overwhelmed with excitement just dropping by your store to window shop. A few will come in just to say "Hi" especially the loyal clients who you have already made friends with. So, it's really effortless establishing rapport with your clients & later on will thrive to friendship you didn't expect come in the package.

People Helping Each Other –
Sounds Great & it Will Be

Furthermore, you also build a network or contacts that will be useful in the future; you never know.

This can be quite a 'personal' kind of business, where you get to know your customers and become familiar with their need, to some extent. Of course as you get busier, there is less time to visit with people – when you've got a line up of people wanting to pay for their purchases – but still time to give a friendly nod or wave to a regular visitor.

Once you start with this interesting business, be sure to always put on a smile & be cheerful to your customers or lookers since they are simply not your customers but potential friends & partners as well.

You Will Get Media Attention

You will be surprised at how much media attention you will get. Anything that is considered "Green" and is directed to reducing the impact humans have on the planet is considered newsworthy.

Since you are doing the planet a huge favor, reporters looking for a "good news story" would not overlook it. It's a wonderful way to see yourself on

T.V., mentioned in newspaper stories, and it certainly will encourage donations, volunteers and shoppers to visit your store.

You Will Earn Respect and Recognition

There are 2 ways you could be possibly seen on the boob tube or be mentioned on newspaper articles. One is via advertisement or promotion of your supported charitable institution. They would even do all the chores for you to get interviews from various media networks and or newspaper companies since it's a noble work for you to donate some proceeds to them & commit a piece of you to them.

Second is because of your loyal customers who cannot stop raving about your thrift shop that it reaches the media. More often that not people become famous through word of mouth. It is a powerful tool to be recognized and appreciated, so to speak. They become your connection & bridge to be heard by the world.

If you want to be famous & be remembered for your benevolence, then you are on the right track. Put up a thrift store & you will never regret the day you invest yourself in this kind of enterprise.

You Will Be Able To Make
Extra Money Selling On eBay

It is somehow understandable for someone to be skeptical to put up a new business since it is a gamble, you might win or lose the game. You never have to worry about a thing because that's why eBay exists.

eBay is for the novice in the ways of the business world, so if you are hesitant putting up your own thrift shop, selling on eBay would be a good secondary income. It is composed of a big network of buyers & sellers who are into buying & selling brand new & vintage stuff. Having an e-store on eBay is a great alternative to having a conventional store. See **eBay University Learning Center** at http://pages. ebaycom/education/selling.html. They provide audio/ visual demonstrations and tutorials to help you get up to speed.

Selling On The Web Really Works!

This is even more cost-efficient since you don't need to rent a space for your store. You just post pictures of your items on line and provide an attractive yet realistic description of these goods & of course a reasonable price so that they will sell like hotcakes. Most of the people that you'll be dealing with on eBay are professionals so they won't normally haggle with the prices.

Soon, you will see how a Bricks and Mortar "real" shop benefits your internet business. A lot of your customers will inquire if you have a shop that they can visit & if you don't have one, they will strongly suggest you to open one.

Many existing businesses such as jewelers, designers, sellers of china dishes and figurines already compliment their income with online sellers such as eBay.

There's no harm in trying especially when it is for free. It won't cost you anything to advertise on eBay, so go ahead & test the waters.

You Will Be Able To Open More Stores And Expand The Business

People Need What You Have To Sell. You can move to a larger location, so more goods can be displayed, or with an experienced and reliable manager, open another store. As you go along, you may want to put in writing some of the expectations and policies that you have built up over time. If you have had a good experience with your current sponsoring charity and they are pleased with your operation, you may choose to remains with the same group.

LAW OF SUPPLY AND DEMAND –
AND YOU ARE IN THE MIDDLE

With a successful thrift store already up and running you have already gained sufficient knowledge about the running your business. It greatly involves the law of supply & demand. Your store becomes very in demand in the market. People are always on the run seeking for more items that you sell and cannot stop talking about your goods. You have no more room for your stuff to be sold since you have a lot of them by now. Instead of not being able to accommodate your customers, opening a new store is really the best bet. Some thrift stores specialize; as in all furniture, or all clothing – which is a great draw for customers who are looking for such particular items.

Since you have achieved your mark in the industry, it would be hassle-free to put up more stores. The market has known you & your satisfactory service so there's no trouble involved here. Besides, people will always need & want what you have to sell one-way or the other.

YOU WILL BE APPRECIATED FOR YOUR
GENEROSITY TO YOUR CHARITY

It is such a delightful feeling to be appreciated for all your hard work even if you are the humblest person on earth. Knowing that your efforts are recognized is already a reward itself. Sort of like the law of karma – what goes around – comes around – just generally saying that when you do somebody a good deed, you will have it done back to you – often many times over.

There are so many worthy charities that need more funds to reach their goals that will impress you with how willing they are to offer you support. They can rally their members to donate, volunteer and shop at your store.

Make a Six Figure Income and Truly Help Others

There is no doubt that your chosen charity would be genuinely grateful for your helping hands. Not only the institution that will be solely appreciative of your assistance but also each person who belongs there will thank you for the rest of their lives for a kind hearted soul that you are. Likewise, your family & relatives will be truly proud of you & your successful thrift shop. This is all because of your creativity to recycle & sell second hand items for a good cause. Anyone would truly brag about you & look up to you.

The incredible Bonus to all this is that you can be making a six figure income, and still be helping the Earth and the sponsoring charity. Your enterprising nature will surely emerge as you build the business and the initial fear you may have encountered (or not) will melt away.

YOU WILL BE PART OF THE BUSINESS COMMUNITY

Having a thrift shop business will meet many of your needs. There will come a time that you would long for a sense of belongingness like it's one of the basic needs of man.

It is always interesting to talk with one's peers and exchange ideas. Service clubs usually encourage entrepreneurs from various business, preferably not those in competition with each other. Networking at these meetings and social events can be very helpful to your business.

YOU WILL HAVE MANY PERSONAL REWARDS AS WELL

Being successful with your store would attract attention from the business community that they would want to know your secrets in the enterprise you are in. These people would ask you tons of questions about your success. In short they would be interested in possibly investing in owning a thrift store too. Since you are the expert, they would love to have you as part of their service clubs & organizations so you can give them more insights / tips, possibly even develop into a franchise business. Moreover, you'll also learn from their business point of views, it will be then an exchange of business expertise & ideas. You'll get to socialize, have cocktails with the elite where you now belong.

Few people realize the secrets to starting and running a high-profit thrift store .

Fortunately you are now one of those people, as you read this book.

No man is an island. Being part of something satisfies a man's cravings whether it is about your personal life or professional life.

THIS TYPE OF BUSINESS HELPS COMBAT GLOBAL WARMING

We are all aware of the hazardous effects of global warming. It is one of the most significant challenges the world is facing. This news is everywhere you look: newspaper, television, Internet etc. But there are always two sides of a coin.

Global warming, destructive does have some advantages to Thrift Store entrepreneurs. These are the folks who are into selling lightly used goods, energy saving appliances and equipment and other cost efficient products.

If you are to own a thrift store, you may not need even to promote it. Customers will be swarming like bees into your shop in no time. They would scout for second hand items since they want to somehow show their concern for the environment and the hunt for a bargain is exciting! Not to mention that some of these customers are fashionistas who don't want to be left out with what's hot & what's not. They love items that are unique & hard to find to keep them in style.

Your Thrift Store Promotes Environmentally Friendly Re-using

You will be astonished that money will come pouring down without much effort on your part. All you need to do is oversee the operations, put on a little smile & be nice to your customers.

Nobody wants climate change but sometimes these kinds of situations bring about business opportunities that are hard to ignore. Adaptability & creativity is the key in surviving this phenomenon, and the business people who recognize this will be the most successful.

Having Your Own Business Improves Your Life

How do you like managing your own time & money? How about having work-life balance in your hands? It's just a preview of the endless joy you could obtain from having your own thrift store.

As the owner of a thrift shop, it is easy for you to have a convenient lifestyle & take pleasure all the wonderful things in life. Being the boss, you can arrange your time off, as you want as long as your store has well trained employees who can take charge while you are away. You can afford to buy things you were just dreaming to have when you were just an employee of some company. Another good point is that you will have more time for other personal matters you want to deal with but just don't have the luxury of it as an employee.

YOUR LIFE WILL CHANGE

You may have wanted to finish the novel that's been sitting dusty in your bookshelf, now is the time to do that. You can now catch up with your friends & be updated with each other's lives. You would not be left out with the current events since you can now have time to know the latest buzz. You can even learn a new skill or craft if you want to.

It all boils down to taking this great chance to improve your professional & personal life. There may be ups & downs with this business like all industries have, nevertheless, it is just a matter of charging your life with optimism & everything will fall into its proper places.

GREEN IS THE WAVE OF THE FUTURE...AND OF NOW

We all know of the 3 R's promoted to help reduce the pollution of our planet: Reduce, Reuse & Recycle. You are definitely one of the driving forces for this worldwide slogan as an owner of a thrift store. Donors want a valid place to give their items to – such as your Thrift Store.

**The 'green' aspect can certainly
be used in your advertising and in
your promotions.**

Of all the 3 R's, you are leading the community or neighborhood towards "Re-use" which is even better than recycling because the item does not need to be reprocessed before it can be used again. This is also known as "growing green" which means using what already exists. This also prevents travel pollution caused by moving newly manufactured goods to your locale.

This Is A Great Time To Be In The Recycling/Reusing Business

People sometimes need a role model or an inspiration to look up to before they realize what needs to be done. You, as a living example of being resourceful; people will be more motivated to re-think about their lifestyles & start to be more planet-friendly. With your shop, you promote re-using of goods & therefore reducing waste from a landfill. When people purchase something from your store, they help prevent climate change even if they are not aware of it. Your store & your customers work hand in hand to conserve resources for the children of the future.

Significantly, it is such a great combination that you encourage creative use of unwanted items & earning a significant income at the same time.

YOU WILL GAIN EXPERTISE FASTER BECAUSE OF WHAT YOU WILL LEARN IN THIS BOOK

You may not have any idea how to go about having a thrift shop of your own. But you never have to worry about a thing. That's what this book is all about.

Using the valuable help from this book will definitely give you an advantage over others who do not have such material to guide them.

This book will address your concern about the advantages of putting up a thrift store. If you need help or motivation, this book will be your companion. It has numerous tips on how to succeed in this kind of business. Sure, experience is the best teacher but it is still advisable to have some background knowledge about something that you're interested in especially if it's about business.

Costly mistakes can be avoided, when you have this help.

This Book Gives You Everything You Need To Be A Success!

Gaining experience, as we all know can be an expensive way to become successful in business. In time you should be accustomed to handling your thrift store on your own because of the lessons you have gained from this book. And you can just keep it as a reference afterwards so you can go back to it anytime you need. Or maybe give it to someone who also wants to run a business like this but is undecided.

You will never go wrong with this book, as it will be your friend who will guide you every step of the way until you reach your goals & become successful in this biz.

PEOPLE WILL ASK TO VOLUNTEER IN YOUR STORE – SAVING ON STAFF COSTS

As soon as you launch your thrift store to the public, acquiring employees should not be an issue at all. Definitely, there would be a lot of people who will offer their services to you.

These people consist of volunteers, unemployed & some senior citizens. For the volunteers who are mostly the youth, you would be able to equip them with the training & overview of the business world. They will learn to be more responsible because of the tasks that they need to accomplish. They will also know the value of professionalism. You also give them the chance to serve the community in their own little way.

Best part is, you'll be saving on employee costs since you don't have to pay these volunteers.

Volunteers Appreciate You and The Experience You Gave Them

Volunteers may ask you for a letter of reference before they apply for a paid job elsewhere. You have provided them with experience; training and can reward their efforts with a recommendation.

For the unemployed, you provide them the chance to earn income again as well as hope to build a bright future for their families.

With regard to senior citizens, some of them may feel unwanted but with job opportunities at your thrift shop, you help them explore their full potentials. Working at your store won't be tough for them. They can always help with simple sorting, hanging, pricing and displaying your merchandise.

This kind of business is really for all types of folks. It captures everyone's capabilities & skills and you even become the instrument of success for these people. What a heartwarming thought!

High expectations are the key to everything.

Sam Walton
Wal-Mart Founder and Businessman

Never be frightened to take a profit. Better in your pocket then theirs.

Michael Levy
Self Help Author

Opening A Thrift Store Will Change Your Life!

How would you like a business that requires a bare bones investment and products that are in such demand that you can start computing profits from Opening Day?

It's Recession Proof And Helps All Sorts Of Other People.

This is a retail business that you have no need to invest a dime in inventory because your inventory is all donated to you, in great volumes, free of charge. A retail business that people will volunteer to work in –to help you and expect little in return?

The business?A for-profit Thrift Store - Selling lightly used clothing, furniture, house wares, electronics dry goods and so on. The nature of this fast growing retail business is so simple but most people have no idea how to create such a thriving business. Moderate estimates put the rate of growth over the last 3 years at between 40%, to over 300% - depending on the operator's expertise and location.

It is not uncommon for individual thrift stores to be expanding at a whopping 100 percent annually. The owner of a for profit thrift store chain in the Midwest opened shop 13 years ago with a few hundred dollars and a few lightly used garments. Two years later she opened a second store, and then another in each of the three following years. She sold three of the stores in her chain at a hefty profit after a few years. The two remaining stores are still going strong and bringing her an annual gross well into six figures.

IMPORTANT TO RE-USE AS WELL AS A REAL NEED FOR BARGAIN HUNTERS

Can you believe that the average North American throws away 67.9 pounds of used clothing and rags into the garbage? This results in over twenty billion pounds (or more than 9.09 billion kilograms) of used clothing and textiles tossed into landfills each year.

When you donate to or shop at a thrift store, you increase the

**re-use of goods and help the
environment. Good on You!**

*Don't be too timid and squeamish about
your actions. All life is an experiment.*

Ralph Waldo Emerson
American Essayist

THRIFT STORES ARE A RAPIDLY INCREASING TREND

Every month there is more and more interest from
entrepreneurs and designers around the world
marketing their green products.

New business are starting up to provide these
products and services and large companies, such
as Wal-Mart, are starting to make green part of
their business strategy. This is just part of a rapidly
increasing trend.

THIS BOOK IS 'MUST HAVE" FOR CHARITIES, ENVIRONMENTALISTS AND ENTREPRENEURS

People looking for a career change, to be their own
boss, and for charities to refer to or use for the
assistance of licensees.

<u>The benefits of being your own boss include:</u>

* use your own talents and skills to develop the
business

- freedom from a boss looking over your shoulder
- increased prestige from having your own business

Painless Fund Raiser For Charities

Charitable organizations will find this book a valuable resource using it as a guide to promote new stores. Give a book to each applicant, to stimulate store growth, encourage recycling and promote increased donations to your organizations.

As more and more non profit groups launch appeals for donations, the donors funds become more and more diluted.

Licensing Thrift Stores to use part of your group's name in return for regular donations is more reliable and is an attainable goal.

This Book Will Enable You To:

1. Rapidly have financial success in your own business Everything you need to start and run a moneymaking Thrift Store is here.

2. Move ahead quickly with your plans to become a successful, respected independent business owner.

3. Excite others, promote and build your business with little cost to you.

4. Pack your new store with donations that are valuable and sought after by eager shoppers.

5. Find cheerful, hard working volunteers to help in the store, and learn how to keep them happy and satisfied.

6. Brighten and encourage other people's day, as you see fit – by donating items from your store.

7. Make a lot of people happy at the charity of your choice with a steady stream of income they would not otherwise have received.

8. Contribute to an important improvement to the environment - reuse, and recycling of goods.

9. Expand your growth and the number of stores, multiplying all of the other positive effects and increasing your personal bank account substantially.

10. Choose a 'dynamite', affordable location for your store.

11. Painlessly arrange financing for your start up expenses.

12. Pick and choose the best merchandise so it sells well.

13. Make a profit from those items that are moving slowly, so as to make room for hot, new goods coming in.

14. Publicize your sponsoring charity, so it gains momentum and raises its profile with the public.

Its All Here – In This Book

This book includes all of the main concerns a for-profit thrift store owner considers - including, what is the right location, a precise overview of your start-up expenses, effective budgeting and planning ,volunteer management, bookkeeping , sample price list and much, much more. Everything about starting and running a thrift shop business that you need to know to vastly increase your wealth .

Starting A Thrift Store
Will Change Your Life For The Better!

An enterprising person is one who comes across a pile of scrap metal and sees the making of a wonderful sculpture. An enterprising person is one who drives through an old decrepit part of town and sees a new housing development. An enterprising person is one who sees opportunity in all areas of life.

Jim Rohn
Business Coach and Motivational Speaker

Chapter 1

Meet the Powerful Need

The Market Is Yours

Consumers have learned that it pays to shop for everything. Cost conscious shoppers will routinely check to see if they can get what they are looking for at a reasonable price. Office workers sometimes use their lunch hour to visit a nearby thrift store – to see if "anything new has come in." Visiting thrift stores can be an exciting adventure for many people seeking to discover a bargain!

People moving to anothercity or neighborhood, willdonate all sorts of clothingand excess household goods.

A friend comments "That must be a new outfit! Its very nice ? Reply – " Thanks – I got it a great thrift shop! Its just like new" common expressions from shoppers who bought a $200 designer jacket for $10.

A main reason thrift stores are growing so quickly is the public's increased awareness of the importance of recycling. Rather than adding their items to land fills, they would much rather donate their unwanted or unneeded items to support a worthy cause.

Environmentally-aware consumers prefer to purchase recycled / reused articles. As well . . . people love to find a bargain!

Consumers are increasingly conscious that thrift store shopping is a wise practical way to get good quality at a huge savings.

Thrift stores have largely evolved from the image of dark, musty junk stores, to more attractive, bright and clean settings.

Most people are not concerned about using previously used items, and appreciate the savings.

Over the last decade, any stigma attached to "buying used" has been replaced with a sense of pride. Shoppers now happily report to their friends and family the terrific items they have discovered at a thrift store, along with almost unbelievable low price.

Shopping for bargains on good, quality clothing and the wide variety of merchandise is a lot more fun and exciting than going to the new- goods- only stores. Thrift stores offer a valuable way to increase their buying power.

SIMPLE SOLUTION – RE-USING IS THE BEST OPTION

Re-using refers to any activity that lengthens the life of an item. But recycling refers to when an item is made over into a new raw material for use in a new product – as in melting down aluminum soda cans and making new ones.

Re-use is an important process of reducing human's impact on the earth.

Re-use is just one of the many benefits a community obtains from a thrift store.

Other positive side effects of the thrift store will be referred to elsewhere in this book.

Why is re-use via thrift stores so important? It reduces the waste of our consumer society and also sustains charitable organizations with financial donations that they would otherwise not receive.

A Window Shoppers Delight!

Reuse Versus Recycle

- Reuse reduces products going to the landfill.
- Reuse saves the energy required to manufacture the item.
- Reusing reduces the air, water and hazardous

waste pollution more than manufacturing a new item.

- Reuse saves on raw materials and transportation pollution.

- Reuse is a great bargain for consumers.

- Reusing and donating to a thrift store generates both new business and jobs.

- Reuse provides a supply of goods that are affordable and accessible.

- Reuse saves the natural resources like trees, and water, causing less disruption to wild animals and endangered species.

It's Already Being Done

Out Of The Closet is a chain of thrift stores in Northern and Southern California owned and operated byAIDS Healthcare Foundation (AHF), the largest specialized provider of cutting-edge medicine and advocacy regardless of ability to pay.

Wary of the high costs of putting on charity events and the volatile nature of donations, they wanted a retail revenue source for the foundation because "the cash register is always ringing." They opened the first Out Of The Closet in Atwater Village in 1990. There are now 20 thrift outlets in California.

Out of the Closet thrift Stores generate 30,000 donations and nearly 1 million shoppers a year.

Out of the Closet sells specialty items through it's eBay auction store. They often receive donations of new designer clothing, film and TV production studios, celebrity memorabilia, exotic collectable's, and more. All of the proceeds from any Out of the Closet Ebay store auction, go to fund HIV medical care.

This Window Tells a Lot to a Passer-By

Enjoy Working With People And Running A Profitable Business?

If you enjoy working with people , are looking for a reliable business with which to spread your wings, you will never regret joining the ranks of for-profit thrift store entrepreneurs who are individually pulling in well over $100,000 annually. A sharp person in this business can make a profit from the first day, and have their investment returned in a matter of a few months. It is common for a new thrift store owner to state that their store was profitable from the first month of operation.

Types Of Thrift Stores

First, there's the thrift store owned and operated by a registered charity. Most people working in a charity are there to help others. They may not be business oriented or even fund raising oriented, which can harm a charity's ability to raise funds and help others.

Some organizations have numerous store locations and report profits in the millions of dollars annually. The larger of these stores may have a paid manager and many volunteers.

Goodwill, and the Salvation Army stores are examples of well run non-profit thrift stores, which have greatly benefited their respective organizations.

This kind of store can be uncomfortable and difficult for a charity group to establish and maintain, as they are not necessarily business oriented, or may already be working flat out to fulfill the charity's goals.

Then there's the entrepreneur owned thrift store that is endorsed by a charitable organization.

The store owner receives the donated goods, and resells it, donating some of the proceeds to the charity. This is commonly an ideal situation for both parties; as the store owner is motivated to make a profit, they will increase the sales and the donation to the charity, freeing it up to do what they do best – help those in need.

The type of resale store that you will be learning about in this book, is the for-profit Thrift Store.

This type of store can carry any type of lightly used clothing, electronics, furniture, home wares, or any type of saleable goods that may be acquired. It will be stocked by donations from the public and have volunteers as its main source of help.

Who Starts Up A Thrift Store?

- An entrepreneurial person with some sales and marketing skills,
- a person who strives to get ahead financially

enjoys helping the community, needs independence, and

- has a desire to help others who may be less fortunate.
- People frustrated with their current careers, maybe because it's a dead-end job
- People who want a stimulating, growing career
- that have ambition and want to be able to develop as they are ready to.
- People who may have had retail experience or even an interest in sales and good customer service.
- People who are unemployed and are looking for a more personally satisfying career.
- People with work experience and organizational skills who recognize the opportunities that a thrift store offers over other types of business.

If you work just for money, you'll never make it, but if you love what you're doing and you always put the customer first, success will be yours.

Ray Kroc
McDonalds Corporation Founder

CHAPTER 2

LOCATION, LOCATION, LOCATION

BEFORE MOVING IN

Thrift shops have appeared in towns with less than 20,000, where the emphasis is less on being formal or fashionably dressed.

Look for signs that indicate that a community is not prospering, with signs such as:

- Sense of defeat or lack of hope amongst community and business leaders.
- High rate of unemployment
- Signs of economic slowness, closed storefronts.
- Unoccupied houses or stores for sale.

AS WELL, YOU MAY SEE POSITIVE SIGNS OF PROSPERITY:

- Attitude of optimism and energy to make the community prosper

- Newly opened bank branches or other chain store
- Attractive landscaping and maintenance of commercial areas
- New construction of office and commercial areas is a positive sign.
- Well maintained or new schools, community centres
- Thriving, active and progressive city government

Located on A Busy Street

PROSPECTIVE SITES

If you find a location in a small business / light industrial area, rents will be somewhat less than in a retail core.

There are three prime 1ocation prospects to consider for this business.

- a storefront in a strip shopping center
- an outdoor shopping mall
- either a small, freestanding building or part of one - near a commercial area

On The Sunny Side Of The Street? – Not Always!

The sunny side of the street is usually not as desirable as the shady side in high-traffic shopping areas.

Merchants on the sunny side of the street often have to install costly awnings to combat the sun and make customers more comfortable. As well, the sun will rapidly fade colors in clothing or upholstered furniture near the windows.

Merchants report that the going home side of the street is usually preferable to the going to work side.

Drivers have the time stop at your thrift store on the way home, versus in the morning when they are in a hurry to get to work on time. Accordingly, it makes sense to make your store's open hours to accommodate people when they are headed home.

What's The Problem? Or Is There One?

It's always good to look into the recent history of a location you like before making a final selection. Some places have had repeated failures, whether due to undetected traffic patterns, or perhaps even the type of neighbours they have. Nearby stores that have a bad reputation can influence the public's choice of whether they even want to go in that area.

Be aware of causes of previous failures so you too can avoid them.

Rent Buys Traffic – And Sales

Locating your store on a busy four-lane street with no median divider in a 30-to-40 m.p.h. zone will allow your customers to turn into your parking lot or park nearby.

As seen by the Starbucks coffee company and other successful chains a corner location is preferred as you take advantage of traffic coming from two directions. Corner locations are sought after for this reason and for the increased visibility.

You can usually get good traffic at outdoor shopping malls as well as lots of parking.

Malls Want Successful Businesses

Mall managers and leasing agents are very conscious of the type of "mix" of businesses they include in the mall. Small malls with 15 to 20 stores will probably not want to bring in any direct competition to the existing tenants. They want to have businesses that thrive in their mall, so that more people visit the various stores, increase everybody's sales and enable the mall owners to be more profitable.

Be Prepared To Impress!

Because of this overall awareness of the shopping center, mall leasing will want a positive concept, your layout design, and at least a first-year pro forma operating forecast, so they can have some confidence of your success. They will have distinct signage requirements and dictate the hours of operation. Malls want consistency, but you may be allowed to extend your open hours, but not reduce them on a regular basis.

In some outdoor malls, as well as paying a monthly rent, you will be asked to report your gross sales. When they exceed an amount agreed upon in the lease you will need to pay them a small percentage of your sales.

While outdoor shopping mall rent is lower than in indoor sites, outdoor malls have the valuable street visibility and access that many indoor malls do not.

Producing a Profit From Day One Isn't Hard to Do.

Having your store in a high foot-traffic area can produce good sales without a lot of advertising. Many thrift shops in general, produce a profit from the day they open the doors.

Mall locations can be very busy, but you will still have a significant growth rate in a high-foot-traffic area. Your real profits will come as you become known to the general public.

Access is an important consideration in determining market area limits.

ZONING CODES

Cities and towns are zone certain areas for specific uses, such as residential, or commercial.

A commercial zone may allow one type of business to operate but not another, so be aware of these restrictions when looking for locations.

CHECK LIST FOR A THRIFT STORE LOCATION:

- Visibility of the store or at least the sign from the street
- Type of neighborhood – you don't want people to feel uncomfortable.
- Zoning of the area
- Amount of traffic that will find it convenient to stop at your store
- Amount of parking available
- Is it on the sunny side of the street?
- Accessibility to potential customers
- History of the site? If there's been a lot of other stores close at that location?
- Is the lease reasonable and flexible?
- What percent of projected income will be used for rent?
- Is it affordable?

Large Yellow Awning Visible for Blocks

*People often say that motivation doesn't
last.Well, neither does bathing..that's
why we recommend it daily.*

Zig Ziglar
Self Help Author of "See you at the Top"

Chapter 3

Leasing

How To Decide On Your Store Size

Your store's physical needs are simple. The size of your store and location are the biggest predictors of your future sales. Affordability is paramount, especially when you first start the store, and the sales and location are unproven to you. 1000 square feet is the smallest practical size. At that size you will not be able to sell furniture – a large profit item. The ideal size for a thrift store is in the range of 2,000 – 4,000 square feet. You will then be able to handle all types of donations – from sofas, dining room sets to figurines. When you are first starting out, its wise to err on the safe side by committing yourself to a smaller area with a smaller amount of rent. At least until you have got the sales volume to move up to a larger area and larger rent.

Thrift stores need to have a parking spot or a loading zone for donations, near the back door if possible. Donors will sometimes arrive with a carload of clothing, electronics, a lawn mower and so on. They need to have easy access to unload these things without delay. Some help from a volunteer of the owner of the business would be courteous and welcomed.

NEGOTIATING TERMS OF THE LEASE

Remember that terms are negotiable, and the time to negotiate is before you sign the lease.

Have your lawyer look the lease over and explain any parts you are not clear on.

These tips will be helpful:

- Have included in writing that the landlord will pay for all constructions or physical changes required for your use.
- Sometimes the landlord will give you a few free months of rent to help close the deal. It's always worth a try to ask for these benefits.
- Rather than arranging a three to five year lease, for example, make an offer for a one-year lease with two additional one-year options. This way you minimize the risk. The location can be less productive than expected, resulting in less

revenue to begin with. On the other hand, if sales are booming you may need to expand your store.

RENTAL PLANNING

Check on realtors, or brokers specializing in commercial rentals in your desired areas. They will help you find the right size and price to suit your needs if they can, but there may be very good locations which are not listed with them. You will be wise to check the local papers for rental opportunities as well. When a professional agent locates a property for you, the owner of the building pays their commission, so it is basically a free convenience for you to use.

KEEPING YOUR COOL WHEN NEGOTIATING

If this is your first business activity, avoid appearing too eager or naïve. There's no harm in staying calm and wary when researching sites. Respectfully negotiating a rental rate is normal and most acceptable in business. Every decrease you can arrange will help you and your sponsoring charity for the present and for the future. You need to state clearly that you are looking for a location for your own business, so there is no misunderstanding that it is on behalf of the sponsoring charity. However, because you will be donating to the charity on a regular basis, depending on sales volume, it can be an important bargaining point for the lessor to consider giving you a favorable rate. Be prepared to state approximately the square footage you are looking for and the rate per square foot you can afford. Having these figures ready will help you to appear confident and businesslike.

Types of Leases

A **net** lease, means that as well as being responsible for paying the fixed rent, your business will be charged part of common property expenses such as utilities, insurance, upkeep and repairs. This will all be written in the lease. Your cost is in proportion to the amount of the total floor space being rented out. For example, if you rent 10 per cent of the shopping centre, the property manager will charge you for 10 per cent of the above-mentioned costs. Leasing managers will routinely provide photocopies of the invoices they pay, so you can be assured these are real costs.

The difference in a gross lease, is that you would pay a gross or fixed amount of rent, each month, which the owner uses as they see fit.

Are You Getting The Lease You Want?

Before signing anything, you and your lawyer need to consider the long-term effect on your business, of restrictions such as the following:

- that restrict the use you intend for the premises,

- that prevent you from making physical changes to your rented space
- You need to be able to sublet or turn your premises over to another business
- Excessive late rental payments penalties or foreclosure rights

Keeping Control of Your Lease Negotiations

It may not always be possible to rent a location on an annual basis but do not feel pressured to accept what's offered to you. There will always be another site opening up elsewhere, perhaps one even better suited for your business.

A big benefit to you is a lease that can easily be assigned to another tenant in case the rent turns out to be too much.

Having this right written in the lease will allow you to close or move your business without penalty or being obliged to remain at the site if you wish not to. You will be able to get another tenant to take over the balance of the lease term.

Selling your business will depend greatly on the terms of your lease. If a buyer doesn't see a clear future for that location, they will walk away. You need to have ensured that your rent will not be raised excessively for your own operation and especially if you plan to sell it.

It is wise to check into any plans the landlord may have for selling the property. A new owner may not be as cooperative, and want a larger return on the investment, resulting in higher rent for you.

You want to run the business and work mainly for your own benefit – not just to pay rent.

Take time to sit down and calculate what costs you could potentially face over the long and short term. Insulate your business as much as possible from threats to your financial well being.

Building Protection Into Your Lease

A lower first year rate, with increases periodically can be helpful to your business. For example, if your rent was $1000 per month for the first 12 months, then perhaps a 5% increase every two years, on a 5 year lease. With another 5 year option for a five year lease, you will have some protection built in to your lease.

Looking Ahead And Being Empowered

Negotiations for the next 5 year period should begin at least 6 months before your existing lease is up and be agreed upon a couple months before the end of the lease. This will allow you time to move if the lessor is asking for too large of an increase. You may need to initiate the negotiations, as the lessor may prefer to leave it until later – giving you less time to prepare to find another more affordable location, or make other changes to better your business. This could be your need for more or less space, improvements or changes that will allow you to best serve your customers.

**Plan for your success. Start off
on the right foot by doing your
"homework!"**

What Can Your Bank Or Credit Union Do For You?

Be aware of the monthly maintenance fee.

Is there is a minimum balance that you must maintain to get free or reduced charges on checks you write?

Is there a fee charged when you make a deposit?

Do they offer online access to your account, so you can quickly confirm deposits, balances and transactions?

Do they support Visa / MasterCard accounts? Business discounts can be negotiable, so compare with other institutions if you plan to offer this service to your customers.

Some institutions offer a package with a monthly fee, which may include: Unlimited in-branch deposits, withdrawals and transfers, and unlimited debit card transactions. These can save you hundreds of dollars over a year.

Quick and easy deposits, which may include tellers exclusively for business deposits. Overnight bag drop off can also be a convenience.

We are upsetting the atmosphere upon which all life depends.

In the late 80s when I began to take climate change seriously, we referred to global warming as a "slow-motion catastrophe" one we expected to kick in perhaps generations later.

Instead, the signs of change have accelerated alarmingly.

David Suzuki
Famous Canadian environmental activist and author

Chapter 4

Tying It Together

Putting Out The Welcome Mat

Good sales in this business depend on a high volume of potential customers visiting your store; you want to do everything you can to encourage people to visit your store.

Foot traffic is always much easier to reach than people in cars. Thrift store shoppers are loyal when they see the fresh merchandise being added to the store regularly. It's very appealing when patrons can park and walk to your door, without obstacles or distance discouraging them.

Before committing to a location, be aware if there is any sort of median divider, or if left hand turns to your store are prohibited during rush hour traffic. This could be a problem if for example left turns are not allowed between 3 pm and 6 pm.

Also if the traffic speed is over 35 mph, cars would have trouble turning into a location with poorly marked entrances and exits. If the parking spaces are always full, that will discourage drivers from visiting your business.

Building Awareness (and Sales!) of Your Store

Even your entrance can be important, it will require wheel chair access and be appealing to customers.

Effective signage, which clearly directs potential customers to your store, can enable people to find you readily. As well print advertising of your location in a local weekly newspaper, especially when starting out, will generate traffic. Usually the sponsoring charity will include news of your location in their newsletters and mail outs. They will usually make mention of your store on their web site, to help increase donations and sales.

Get acquainted with the neighborhood you are considering. For example, you can park in the area and watch the foot and vehicle traffic at various times of the day. Speaking to nearby business owners, asking them about their satisfaction with the area, will turn up lots of interesting information that may otherwise be unavailable. When you have clear, large signage, so that people notice your store, it will become somewhat of a destination, even in a lower traffic area. People like to donate their clothes and items they no longer use, to a good cause, and have them recycled, rather than toss them into the garbage. Bargain hunters will be delighted to discover your store and become regular shoppers as long as you keep rearranging the merchandise and putting out new items.

KNOW YOUR COMPETITION AND YOU'LL BEAT THEM!

Attempt to identify the competitors in your area and their specialties. Study their style and method of operation, how long they have been in business, their marketing strategy, how much they charge, and their clientele.

If they are successful, try to ascertain why and use this information to determine how you can best distinguish yourself and find your niche in the market. You want to know what makes your style unique if a prospective client were to compare you and your competitors.

Sometimes there may be several thrift stores in a city block. Don't be shy about meeting them. You are not enemies, just because you are in the same business. That's a good reason to be cooperative and helpful to each other. Call one at a time and set a coffee date at a nearby coffee shop to meet each other and go and meet them. A coffee shop is neutral territory; so neither of you need feel threatened by being in the other person's space.

Be friendly - they may have heard incorrect statements about you or your business, so you can clarify these things and attempt to establish a friendly business relationship. Just the fact that you initiated the coffee date (with no hidden agenda) will favorably impress your competitors.

SELLING ON THE WEB

There are many opportunities for selling goods on the Internet. They all have some sort of fee structure and require you to package and ship the item, but there are good safe ways of getting paid, including Paypal. com, which is owned by eBay. PayPal lets you send money to anyone with email. It is free for consumers, and works seamlessly with your existing credit card and current account. www.paypal.com.

Here Are Some Of The Main Sites:

There are lots of procedures to learn, so pick one place to sell the item and stay with it until you feel comfortable trying another one.

www.Amazon.com/marketplace

If you're planning to sell in volume, see their Pro Merchant Quick Start Guide. If you sell in volume and sell items other than books, music, videos, or DVD's review their Selling on Amazon program.

www.ebay.com

eBay is mainly an auction site, where you can submit a description and a photo of the item for sale; you can set the lowest price you want, without the buyer's knowledge and list how long you want to have it be for sale. At the end of that period, you can accept or reject the offer if it is below your preset limit.

Any reputable seller that needs to liquidate excess inventory can sell in the Reseller Marketplace.

www.ubid.com

uBid is an online auction house with a very large range of products.

Visit other ebay locations as well:

www.Half.com

WWW.Kijiji.com

www.ProStores.com

www.Rent.com and

www.Shopping.com

For more specialized auction sites, you can use www.Google.com, www.Yahoo.com, or www.ask.com to find almost anything you are looking for on the Internet.

Gaining Business From Your Sign

Your exterior sign is an important contact between your thrift shop and passersby. It's a strong communication with your potential customer. It needs to be bright and conspicuous enough to attract attention without being garish. Usually a simple "Thrift Shop" is enough to convey the message, without detracting from its main goal of inviting consumers to come in and save money.

Putting up a large, professional-looking sign that can be seen easily from all directions, with one or more lights illuminating it is all that is needed.

When your sign looks professional, potential customers get the impression that your store is also well run.

Nobody Can Miss This Great Sign!

CHOOSING AN AFFORDABLE FLOOR PLAN

Successful thrift shops have been started in areas as small as 1,000 square feet and as large as 4,000 square feet. Some operators who opened shop initially in 1,000 square feet have seen their business rapidly outgrow its location. They were deluged with donors who came to unload their clothing, furniture and electronics until they soon didn't have any space for new inventory as it arrived.

The best size for a first-time store, complete with retail and receiving areas, is from 1,200 to 2,000 square feet.

It has to be affordable for you – that is most important.

Use as much space as possible for retail space - if the customers can't see it, they can't buy it.

You will need a small office/storage space — to handle shipping and receiving, storage. You can always go vertical, when it comes to storage – using cabinets and shelves. Some attractive thrift shops have shelving on every wall. This keeps breakables out of harm's way and creates a lot of valuable display area for dishes, toys, small electronics plus whatever else you have had donated.

EQUIPPING AN OFFICE

To keep costs down, buy secondhand furniture to start your office.

There are certain basic things you need for your office, including desk, chairs, bookcases, file cabinet, calculator, telephone answering machine. You will probably need a computer, printer, photocopy/fax machine.

A basic desktop computer or laptop will be all you need, to keep records, do bookkeeping entries, or set up files.

EQUIPMENT

A small desk, a chair, and a couple of filing cabinets will start you off. You can probably get by for under $500 if you buy used furniture and shop around for it.

Thrift stores are not complicated businesses, so keep it simple.

Don't be in a hurry to buy these things, if you have a choice, as you will have them donated, and save yourself more money. If needed in the beginning – buy them used, like your customers do.

A counter of about 36 inches on the sales clerk's side will provide a working surface for running the cash register, wrapping items, and writing out sales slips. Shelves under the counter provide space for storing business forms, receipts and other supplies.

Most of the fixtures you'll need in the beginning are available from local suppliers. Your phone company's Yellow pages can be helpful to find the fixtures. Try looking under: used store accessories, used accessories or store accessories.

Buy used goods whenever possible – racks, shelves and other fixtures will be donated in time, so keep your costs to the minimum. Sometimes fixtures from retail stores that have closed may be available for low prices. On the Internet, sites such as **craigslist. org** have an abundance of good used items for sale in your city. Or you can post a free ad on Craigslist telling the public what you are looking for.

Can't live without – a professional Fabric Steamer – faster and easier than ironing – inexpensive. - makes garments, upholstery look like new. No chance of damage like there is with an iron.

FREE BUSINESS SOFTWARE

There is no charge for downloading and using programs on OpenOffice.org, but they do accept donations to help maintain the services.

OpenOffice.org has made available its free office suite for Windows, Mac and Linux. The OpenDocument format can be used by any office application without fear of vendor specific lock-in or onerous licensing terms and fees, with the confidence that documents can be viewed, edited and printed for generations to come.

Users can download it for free from the Project's Web page at http://download.openoffice.org/2.0.0/index.html.

Their website says the programs are easy to learn and use by even the most inexperienced user. It is available in more than 60 languages. These programs are increasingly the choice of businesses and governments throughout the world. Earlier versions have been downloaded over 49 million times since the project's inception

A V<small>OICE</small> M<small>AIL</small> <small>SYSTEM</small>

This can be particularly useful in your business – if you are busy with a customer, and already multi-tasking, let the answering system take the message and return the call as soon as possible.

Phone companies have a range of affordable business services that can greatly add to your customer service and enhance the image of your store.

Here is an overview of some of the more popular choices:

Call Display - See your caller's name and number.

Call Waiting Deluxe - Can have five options to choose how to handle incoming calls with a touch of a button.

- Switch between calls just like regular call waiting
- Send a caller directly to your voice mail
- Send a caller a "please hold" message
- Conference a caller in with your current call
- Take a new call
- A special ring will alert you to an incoming long distance call

Call Forwarding - Automatically forwards calls to any number you choose.

Voice Mail - Takes messages even when you're on the phone or internet.

Visual Call Waiting - See who's calling while you're on the phone.

Call Director - Send a message to your waiting caller while you're on the phone.

Call Screen - Block out the calls you don't want.

Call Transfer - Allows you to transfer a call from your telephone to an external telephone number or mailbox.

Selective Call Waiting - Say goodbye to unwanted phone interruptions.

Internet Call Director - Manage your calls from your computer while you're on the Internet.

Per Call Blocking - Prevents your name and number from being displayed when you call someone who has Call Display.

Custom Ring - Know who the call is for before you answer.

3 Way Calling

Dial Lock - you control the type of toll calls permitted from your phone system. Automatically block outgoing calls to long-distance numbers, including pay-per-call (900) and international numbers. Also block operator-assisted, or directory assistance calls.

TIP – these features all cost you money. You may need some or none of them. Enter the potential costs into your budget first to see what you can afford.

If you want more, you have to require more from yourself.

Dr. Phil McGraw
Motivational Author and Talk Show Host

Chapter 5

Making The Store's Interior Inviting And Practical

Decorating

Thrift stores tend to need little or at least simple decorating. This does help reduce start up costs as well as ongoing maintenance. You may want to hang products from the walls, or mount shelves along the walls, to maximize use of all the space. A fresh coat of paint can go a long way to brightening up a space.

Lighting And Fixtures

Rows of fluorescent lighting fixtures are best and will help lower your power bill.

Make sure you have enough lighting. Your merchandise needs to be on display to be purchased. Most people who are experienced thrift store clothing shoppers are not looking for décor nor atmosphere.

But if your store is dark or poorly lighted, it can discourage potential customers.

Here, store fixtures refers mainly to such items as, indoor lighting, checkout counter, clothes racks, tables, , wall systems, and showcases for product display.

Shoppers like to see their potential purchases as being close to new. Nobody wants to be reminded of the previous owner in any way.

1. Clothing Racks (5 needed at $150-$300)

2. A used glass fronted and topped display case for small or costly items.

3. Pegboard, for easily hanging almost anything from the wall – from purses, handbags, to clothing.

4. Shelving, for along the wall, to display toys, personal items. Sturdy, well braced shelving for the books. Books are heavy and will bend or break casual shelving.

5. Full-Length Mirrors inside and outside the change rooms.

6. Checkout Counter

7. Change rooms for trying on clothes. Can be simple, with a curtain pulled across for privacy, a couple of clothes hooks to hang garments on, and a chair or bench.

8. Vacuum cleaner, floor and window cleaning equipment with supplies.

9. Lint brushes, will help merchandise look better ,and sell faster.

10. A small portable steamer is useful to quickly get rid of wrinkles from clothing

11. Hangers – should be of good quality – heavier plastic for instance, causes less tangle and a lot less straightening and sorting out than wire hangers do. A garden hose or big, deep sink is convenient to freshen up some dusty merchandise .

INTERIOR SIGNAGE HELPS YOUR CUSTOMERS

As simple as possible – eye-catching, with contrasting letters and background – dark blue or green painted sign on white background - that covers as wide an area that is obvious to the most traffic. The public is so saturated with outdoor advertising, and signs – they can miss noticing all but the obvious.

Note: You can buy hangers with easily visible color or letter coding on them. For example a red, blue or yellow ring built into the upper body of the hanger, so the size of the garment is easy for the shopper to see. You can have a small sign nearby, indicating what size each color represents.

KEEP YOUR MERCHANDISE MOVING – AND BUYERS HAPPY!

In order to keep your merchandise fresh and current, you can attach a different color tag (or even a sticker or a thread) for every month to identifying items that are not selling.

You can put it on a Final Sale rack for a couple of weeks, and if it is still not sold, some major thrift stores will purchase used clothing from you by the pound.

After a pre set time, maybe 30 – 60 days all you have to do is check the floor for a certain color of tag used two months ago and clear all the merchandise marked with those tags off the floor. Unless you keep putting out new items, shoppers will lose interest and stop visiting your store. A lost customer is a terrible and preventable thing.

Advertising costs as well as sales will be wasted if you don't give shoppers the bargains they want.

You will also need a good supply of paper or plastic bags to use for sales. Recycling pre-used bags is fine – no need to buy any. Some supermarkets or department stores may well have outdated new bags they would be glad to give you, just to get them ou8t of their storage..

Tagging Equipment not needed – as it saves a lot of time and money to post the prices on a chalkboard on the wall, for customers to refer to.

Floor Plan Layout For Top Sales

Depending on the size, a thrift store's layout is important. If it is a small store, say 1,000 square feet, the whole store will visible to the customer when they walk in. Small round clothing racks are versatile for a store this size. They allow easy access to the customer and are small enough to be moved around the store when empty to accommodate other displays as needed.

For the larger stores, with perhaps higher shelves, restricting the view, you can place your best selling items in the front third. This will help attract, shoppers walking by and will be drawn into the store. Ladies blouses and attractive dresses should be placed here, along with a mannequin dressed in an eye catching outfit. The middle third of the store should be your next best sellers like toys or novelty items, and the least profitable items should be in the back third men's clothing more casual clothing.

Pay attention to your aisles, keeping them clear and clean.

Normally, the space nearest the store entrance will deliver the highest volume of sales

MAKING YOUR STORE INTERESTING AND ENJOYABLE TO VISIT

Use the following guidelines:

Wide, open aisles encourage your customers to spend time browsing the merchandise. You can mix up the line of products by putting a display on an aisle end or even in an aisle, causing a partial obstacle. This method promotes interest and makes a suggestion for an item the shopper may have not otherwise have noticed.

Slow selling goods can be located in the rear of the store.

You can make a little 'library' section, with shelves of books.

Small whimsical or impulse items should be located near the cash register. Jewelry and china figurines must be in the glass display case, for security.

Moving racks or shelves of items can cause them to be noticed by shoppers who may have overlooked them previously. Even moving individual pieces of merchandise will have a "new look" in a new location.

Before putting an item on the sales floor, be sure it is clean and as presentable as possible. I recently visited a popular thrift store; saw a nice looking vacuum cleaner for a good price. When I opened it up to see if it was a bag less type or not, there was a full bag of dirt inside! Psychologically it suddenly became unattractive yuck – who needs somebody else's dirt!

SALES AWARENESS – SHAMELESS PROMOTION!

Everything depends on your sales! Keep that in mind with every decision you make concerning the layout of your store. ITS ALL ABOUT SALES! Operating a thrift store can be distracting at times, where there are lots of activities going on – keeping the merchandise in a presentable appearance, managing the volunteer staff, pleasing the customers. But unless you are concentrating on getting customers into your store EVERY DAY, nothing else will matter. You have to make a profit to stay in business.

SELF EXAMINATION

Are you doing the things that are best for you? Will you make the business a success?

> *I think along the way, as we treat nature as model and mentor, and not as a nuisance to be evaded or manipulated, we will certainly acquire much more reverence for life than we seem to be showing right now.*

> Amory Loving
> American Environmentalist

Chapter 6

Partnering For Success Is The Key!

A Win-Win Deal!

Usually, the entrepreneur enters into an agreement with a charitable organization of his/her choice, to donate a certain percentage of sales to the charity. Because it is a for profit business, there has to be at least a reasonable profit for the operator. By entering into some sort of agreement, it quickly becomes a win-win situation. Members of the community donate saleable goods to the thrift shop, in order to offer support to the charity, the goods are sold, helping many people in the community who may not otherwise have access to such values – the charity gets cash donated help it – and the operator takes home a good profit! Which encourages and enables him/her to continue offering the service.

Charities are sometimes unaware of the revenue they can collect from the thrift shop using their name.

One charity spokesperson said of their relationship with a for profit thrift shop which advertised that he made donations to the charity; "Oh he just makes a donation to us every month, we don't have any particular agreement." Apparently, this arrangement was working satisfactorily for

Treasure Cottage North Vancouver Thrift Store
Proud to be supporting SOS Children's Village B.C.
Donations of gently used items always welcome and accepted at rear of building

Sign Clearly Requests Quality Donations

both parties, even though it seems quite casual and possibly unstable for the charity.

Finding a sponsor – who you will both be happy with - a win-win situation.

Your Relationship With Your Sponsor Charity

Make arrangements with your charity to be able to issue tax receipts for larger donations. For example if a donor brings in a sofa that will sell for $200.00 you will be able to issue tax receipt for that amount. You can advertise this benefit and increase donations. Sometimes you may be able to assist a person who has few worldly possessions with a set of clothes to get them started – or of helping a single parent who needs clothes for their kids to go back to school.

Negotiations with your sponsoring charity – make sure you don't promise more than you can deliver.

Don't be intimidated by the people working for the charity. Their job is to make the best arrangements for their organization, so don't take the discussions personally. The most important thing to remember is that no matter what, you have to keep the doors to your thrift store open. There are many charities who would love to have regular donations, so if you encounter a person representing a charity who seems to think they are doing you a big favor by lending their name to your store, maybe it is time to move on.

While these are your personal decisions and you can't give to everyone, they can be very satisfying for you. Occasionally you may be able to donate some office furniture to your sponsoring charity, if they are opening an additional office.

These examples are not obligations, but opportunities to help others as you see fit. As well, word of your generosity will become known and repaid to you.

Good Two Way Communications are Essential

Keep the lines of communication open! Have one person that you can report any news to – either by email or voice.

You want to keep that person informed on the progress of your store, and make them look good to their boss, the board of directors or to their peers. It really is a win-win position for you and your sponsoring charity.

CHOOSING A CHARITY TO WORK WITH

Be aware of the public image of the organization. Occasionally a charity has had scandals if the funds they collect are not used in an acceptable manner. Some groups have been accused of spending most of their funds on administration and executive salaries.

You have the right to ask to see the charity's financial statements and see proof of the percentage of the funds that goes directly to the programs the charity exists to fund.

Give the public everything you can give them, keep the place as clean as you can keep it, keep it friendly.

Walt Disney
The Walt Disney Company

Chapter 7

Tailoring The Business To Fit You!

Legal Options

(Disclaimer – This is not legal or accounting advice. Please consult a professional)

Sole Proprietorship

A sole proprietorship is the simplest and least expensive method of starting a business. A minimum or no legal requirements are required to except to start the business.

Check with you professional advisors before opening the business, so you get accurate advice for your area.

A sole proprietorship means that you personally will be responsible for all debt of your company, but lenders require your personal guarantee in any case, so its not a big drawback.

Partnership

A partnership of two or more people is possibly the most difficult type of business arrangement.

This is because each partner is liable for the other's actions. If there is ever a legal or credit problem, each partner is equally vulnerable.

If one partner leaves, or declares bankruptcy the other partner is left holding the bag.

The partner with the most to lose personally usually gets hit the hardest.

Partnerships seldom thrive or even survive without a lot of conflict. Partners frequently decide to close the business, rather than continue in an unhappy relationship.

Corporation

The company alone is legally responsible for its actions and debts. You are personally protected in most situations, since you will be an employee of the corporation only, even though you may own all or most of the stock.

You will still have to accept personal liability for any corporate loans made by banks or other financial institutions.

Normally included is an agreement determining the price of a selling shareholder's shares if the remaining shareholders wish to purchase them, or it might grant the other shareholders the right of first refusal. Usually a time period of 30 days, for example is included for how long other shareholders have to purchase the outstanding shares. After that period, the shares may be purchased by an 'outsider' with or without other shareholder's agreement.

More Money In Your Pocket - Keep Your Receipts

The only disadvantage is potential double taxation because the corporation must pay taxes on its net income, and you must also pay taxes on any dividends you may receive from the corporation. However, there are many business related deductions that may be used to reduce the amount of tax payable.

You Need A Raise? You Are The Boss!

As well, sometimes business owners may increase their own salaries in order to reduce or wipe out corporate profits and thereby lower the possibility of having those profits taxed twice (once to the corporation and again to the shareholders upon receipt of dividends from the corporation).

Your professional accountant and lawyer are the best source of

information to custom fit the most suitable arrangement for your situation.

Whatever route to incorporation you may choose, be certain that the forms are accurately and fully completed before submitting them. You wouldn't want to suddenly learn that you have been unsuccessfully registered in some way and have to pay a much higher tax rate.

Now, You Get To Choose Your "Stage" Name

Sole proprietorships and partnerships may choose a distinctive name for their businesses.

Procedures vary. In many states, you need only go to the county offices and pay a registration fee to the county clerk. Other states require placing a fictitious name ad in a local newspaper.

Finding Out Is Not Hard To Do

The easiest way to determine the procedure for your area is to call your bank and ask if it requires a fictitious name registry or certificate in order to open a business account. If so, inquire where you should go to obtain one. Don't be shy - you can learn a lot, just by asking questions. If one person doesn't know, ask if they can recommend where else you can search.

Fictitious name filings usually do not apply to corporations unless the corporation is doing business under a name other than its own. Documents of incorporation have the same effect for corporate businesses as fictitious name filings have for sole proprietorships and partnerships.

Choosing a fictitious name should reflect what type of business you are operating. You can choose a word or two of the sponsoring charity's name as long as it does not misrepresent your business nor infringe on the charity's name.

Licenses And Permits

Most cities and counties require business operators to obtain various licenses and permits to show compliance with local regulations.

License To Do Business - And To Make Money!

City business license departments are required to ensure that your business meets the safety and zoning requirements of that region. They must ask pertinent questions to ensure all businesses operate within the city by-laws. You simply pay a fee to operate your business in that city.

As well, your sponsoring charity will want to be assured that your

business is operating within the law in all ways.

Building inspections and drawings of layout of the store floor plan may be required. They don't expect you to be an artist, so just do your best to illustrate your plan.

Your application for a license will be checked by the planning or zoning department, to confirm the zone covering your property allows the proposed use and that there are enough parking places to meet the code.

If you are opening your business in an existing structure that previously housed a similar business, it should be straightforward.

Just SIGN Here

Most areas have sign ordinances that restrict the size, location, and sometimes the lighting and type of sign used. Landlords may have certain requirements as well, particularly if you leasing area in a mall.

To be on the safe side, check with City Hall and secure the written approval of your landlord before you invest in a sign.

Be sure to include a readable size lettered sign stating that this store is independent of the Charity it makes donations to.

SAFETY FIRST – YOUR FRIENDLY LOCAL FIRE FIGHTERS

Usually, your local fire departments will require your business to obtain a permit from them if customers or the public at large will occupy your premises.

Fire officials can ask at any time to inspect your premises, to ensure you are meeting all the requirements. You need to have the street number of your location displayed in easy to read numbers in an obvious place. Usually it is over or on the main entrance where the public is most likely to look first.

If your street address is not clearly marked, emergency services may have to waste time reacting to an emergency call from you.

The most common problems are blocked exits and charged fire extinguishers not being up-to-date. These bylaws are for your protection as well, so its good operating practice to set a routine for watching these safety precautions.

We simply must do everything we can in our power to slow down global arming before it is too late. The science is clear.
The global warming debate is over.

Arnold Schwarzenegger
Famous actor turned American politician.

Chapter 8

Merchandise And Money

Stocking Up Before The Opening

Before your store opening, have your sponsoring charity request its members to bring donations of whatever they can to your store. –

> **You may even put a "teaser" ad in the local paper – Opening Soon – donations and volunteers needed along with your address, etc.**

Other thrift stores that are not in your neighborhood (so they are not direct competition) will often sell you some of their excess donations, which have not been picked over. Other stores may have many bags of clothing donations, which they will sell you for a few dollars each. You will soon have a lot of donations; so don't spend much money buying goods.

You do want to open with a full looking store or shoppers may be disappointed in your selection and not come back.

THE 'SOFT OPENING'

You should be selling merchandise for a few weeks before your Grand Opening. This will help get the volunteers and you adjusted to having the store open, working efficiently and fixing any procedures that may cause disorganized.

Your business sign(s) should be up as should most - or your entire inventory in the store.

**Customers will wander in and
word of your wonderful bargains
will spread quickly.**

During the Grand Opening, if you decide to go that way, have some drawings for door prizes (take a photo of the winners and publish for advertising). Gift certificates for your business are always handy.

Have supplies of business cards, sponsoring charity brochures, gift certificates, and specialty advertising items in the store.

Coffee, snacks, and other refreshments will add to the festive mood.

ACCEPTING DONATIONS –
AND HOW THEY WILL KEEP COMING IN!

Make your merchandise sparkle with customer appeal! Clean, fresh merchandise will get you the best return:

Clothing items must be clean and fresh smelling. A quick steaming will get you the best price.

For household items, a dusting will brighten them up. Glass items must be clean and not chipped or cracked. Spending a moment to look it over carefully before it goes on sale is a good investment of your time.

When you receive a set of dishes, puzzles or games - make sure no parts are missing.

Your time is valuable, but when able to make a small inexpensive repair, it will increase the selling price and sell faster.

Oh – and please don't forget to say "Thank You" sincerely to each and every donor. They bring generosity and goodwill to your store – and deserve your attention.

INCREASING DONATIONS

If you want something —just ASK – let others know.
Whether its Donations, increased Sales, Volunteers
– and you will have as many as you want. Once the
existence of your thrift store becomes known in your
community, you will have no shortage of donations.
Many for-profit thrift stores seldom advertise of
promote – relying instead on walk in traffic.

PICKING UP DONATIONS

Set certain day(s) for Pick-up Service – mainly for
large pieces, or a large quantity of clothing and other
goods. If you don't have a large enough truck in the
beginning, to handle 4 – 6 pieces of furniture, you
may want to rent one locally, until revenue provides
adequate profit to afford one.

ISSUING RECEIPTS

Tax receipts are a big incentive for donors to choose
to give to your thrift store. You can set a minimum
selling price as a guide for the amount to issue a
receipt. Discuss with your sponsoring charity what
they would consider acceptable. Some stores offer
receipts only when the donation will sell for $200
or more. This decision is up to the charity, as any
receipts will be issued only in their name, with their

approval, even though your store can be doing the actual assessment and handing out the receipts.

Layaway

Short term layaway is a service you may want to offer some customers who want to buy a large item or a number of items amounting to a large dollar amount.

Usually, layaways work out just fine. The customer may not come back to finish paying for the order. Then you could be stuck with merchandise you might have been able to sell outright. It is in your best interest to put a time limit and minimum deposit on layaways. A 50-percent deposit and a 30-day limit (or less) are fair.

Make sure your sales clerks clearly explain the terms to your customers, so the buyer is not disappointed if the order is taken off layaway and sold.

Getting their phone number is helpful, so they can be given a short courtesy call to remind them that their order is waiting to be paid for & picked up.

Write the person's name & phone number on the bag, with the date purchased and amount already paid. Laying away orders for customers can be a bit of a nuisance, so provide the service only rarely and for orders over a set amount, say $50.00

Accepting Checks

We suggest that you post your check-cashing procedures in a highly visible place. Most customers are aware of the problem of bad checks and are willing to follow your rules. But if your rules are not known until the customer reaches the check stand (for example, that you require two forms of identification), it can cause ill feelings.

Your main reason in asking for identification is to locate the customer if something is wrong with the check. The most valid and valuable piece of identification is a driver's license, which in most states gives a picture, signature and address. If the signature, address and name agree with the check, you are probably safe.

It is possible to get insurance against bad checks from such companies as Telecredit Inc. Typically, such a check-reporting service charges a fee for check verification, usually 4 to 6 percent of the face value of the check. This depends on the size of your operation, hence volume of checks you send through the system. If you called in a $600 check, for example, the service would cost you $24. However, weigh that charge against the possibility of losing the $600 completely, and the service has merit.

If you are not connected with one of these check-verification systems, you should ask for a second piece of identification—check guarantee card, bank card, or a shopping plate. Retail merchants' associations often provide lists of stolen driver's licenses, credit cards, and shopping plates, so if the customer is unknown to you, it makes sense for you to check the list.

CREDIT CARDS

By accepting credit cards like VISA and MasterCard, you enable your customers to charge their purchases directly through the bank. This eliminates the procedures required for you to grant credit to a customer.

To avoid making deposits at more than one bank each day, look for one that handles these two major cards.

In case you are not familiar with the procedure for handling credit card sales, here's how it works: You deposit the credit card sales draft in the bank just like a check. The bank deducts a service fee, (which can be negotiated, depending on the size usually 3 or 4 percent of the face amount of the sales draft, and credits the balance to your checking account. Therefore, the sale is almost like a cash sale.

The charge to the specific firm will vary with two basic factors: 1) total volume of credit card sales and 2) the average dollar sale. An airline that discounts $2 million per week with a credit card company and has an average sale of $100 may pay a charge of 1 percent.

It's ironic that retailers and restaurants live   or die on customer service,   yet their employees have some of the lowest   pay and worst benefits of any industry.   That's one reason so many retail experiences   are mediocre for the public.

Howard Schultz
American entrepreneur and chairman of the
Starbucks coffee chain of stores.

CHAPTER 9

RUNNING THE STORE

PHONE MANNERS

Using the telephone for personal and at your thrift store business is so common, most people assume they have good manners on the telephone.

This is not always true, so I'll go over some points on how to use the telephone to make you and your business look good and develop skills to.

The way the phone is answered makes an important first impression—hopefully always good.

First time callers in particular, form a strong impression about your company on their experience with that first phone call. Callers have only your attitude and the tone of your voice, to judge your business by. All the caller knows about your company is influenced by the person who answers your business

, so it is important to make it a positive experience for your potential customer.

Besides, you may be amazed by the response you get when being friendly and courteous – so often callers give you back the same attitude you give them, making it an enjoyable time for both persons involved.

Here are some tips to sounding good and creating the type of impression you want:

Smile when answering the telephone. This may feel silly at first, but your voice will sound friendly, professional, and enthusiastic. Think of a friend on the other end of the phone, to make it feel more natural

Tell the caller:

1. name of business,

2. your name and

3. ask how you can help them.

Try not to speak too quickly, and do clearly pronounce the words. This will save you both time and confusion.

It's a good idea to keep a notepad and pencil near the phone so you can make notes during the conversation. This will help you to be accurate and avoid having to ask the caller to repeat himself or herself. Particularly if they are calling about having you pick up some furniture or if they want to know a good time to deliver donations.

Try to answer promptly, by the second or third ring unless you are already involved with a customer. Otherwise your phone answering system will take over and either give the call the information they want, such as your hours of operation, or give them a chance to leave a message, which you can call back about when you are able. Don't put off returning the call, they could become impatient and make a valuable donation to someone else if they feel you are not attentive.

Listen carefully to what the caller is saying.

Callers may feel you do not value their call if you are not listening and responding appropriately. If you must put someone on hold, ask for and receive their permission first. Try to make the delay as brief as possible, and then thank them for holding, when you return to their call.

Always finish the conversation with a positive tone. Before ending the conversation, check with the caller that they are satisfied with your conversation and ask if there is anything else you can do for them.

If they have given you their phone number, address, name - repeat the caller's information, and nature of the call to confirm you have written it correctly.

When ending the call, it's easy to get into the habit of thanking them for calling,and adding whatever pleasantries feel comfortable and natural for you.

Voice Mail

Keep your outgoing message current. For example, having a recording about a special Christmas Promotion going on in the month of July will lead the caller to think you are not paying attention to the business.

When you leave a message for someone, make it as detailed as possible, without dragging it out too much or saying, "Please give me a call." Speak slowly and clearly, including the best time to call you back.

Using Voice Mail To Your Benefit

Experts say 3 out of 4 business calls are not completed on the first attempt. The effect is an incredible amount of wasted time and energy. To reduce telephone tag, when recording an answering machine message you can ask people to leave a detailed message and say when you expect to be able to return their call.

It often helpful to callers if you give the store hours, street address, give pick up times as well as the choice for them to leave a detailed message.

Ask that phone messages mention what the call was about, so you can take care of it more quickly and delegate if possible. Set a couple of times each day to return calls so that they are not disrupting your work.

Call-Waiting

Personally, I have discontinued call waiting on my phone. I think it's impolite and aggravating to the caller to continually put the person who originally called - on hold while you take another call. It is also stressful to you, to be balancing callers in that manner.

To eliminate this situation, I use a voice mail service to take any incoming calls while I am on the phone. This way I can focus on the caller and treat them with the respect and attention they deserve.

CUSTOMER SERVICE

Many thrift shop customers can well afford new clothes but feel their prices are higher than they want to spend. Avoid any generalizations or prejudice about your customers.

Each and every person who enters your store is entitled to your respect and courtesy, regardless of their perceived level of income.

Parents of children find thrift shops are a great answer to the expense of buying children's clothing that are outgrown rapidly, often in only a few months.

An important way to have repeat customers is to treat every person's purchase as something important. All customers are valued, whether they spend $5 or $1,000.

BE FRIENDLY! IT FEELS GOOD TO YOU AND TO THEM

Its good business to acknowledge each person that enters your store, preferably with a smile and pleasant greeting, even if you are already with a customer. It sets the friendly, helpful tone for the customer's experience in your store . As well by greeting and making eye contact with each potential customer, they feel as though you are interested in them.

You'll do better by emphasizing service in your store not aggressive sales. People may resist sales efforts and not come back if they feel pressured to buy. They want to be able to browse the merchandise, rather than being "sold." They do appreciate help and assistance when they want it, for example when trying to find a certain size or color.

Front Line People Make the Impression – to Buy or Not

Whoever greets a customer or answers the store phone is the only impression made to your customers. Volunteers / staff need to be reminded how extremely important their role is.

There will always be an occasional angry or unhappy customer.

First thing to remember is that it is not personal. You are not being attacked, even though it may seem as though you are.

Keeping your calm is important, so as not to inflame the situation and so you can find out how you can help the upset customer and make them pleased enough to come back and shop at your store again.

Treating the customer with the same respect and dignity that you would want to be treated with, will go a long ways to resolving the customers complaint.

HEY GOOD LOOKING!

Your personal appearance is vitally important to creating a respectable image for your business. The main items to consider are that your clothes fit reasonably well, are neat and clean. Your hair needs to be clean and tidy so that you are able to assist customers and have them feel comfortable.

Your vehicle for picking up donations needs to normally be spotlessly clean. This vehicle represents your business and will influence how the community regards your business.

I think along the way, as we treat nature as model and mentor, and not as a nuisance to be evaded or manipulated, we will certainly acquire much more reverence for life than we seem to be showing right now.

Amory Lovins
American Environmentalist

Chapter 10

Tips and Tricks

Profiting From Time Management

Here are a some helpful time management tools that are easy to put into practice.

Make a List of Your Priorities

Decide which ones are high, medium and low priorities. Write them down.

- Then list them as 'A' for items that are most important to you and your business.
- List as 'B' the Medium-priority tasks that are not as important, as the "A' chores, and may be delegated.
- Listing a task as 'C' will indicate low priority items that need to be done, but are not as immediate as the other priorities.

Each day before leaving work, you can write down a quick list of "to do" items for tomorrow.

This will give you immediate direction as soon as you get to work.

Keeping such a list will give you satisfaction and feeling of progress – as items are crossed off. It will also reduce stress that results from trying to remember everything that has to be done. When you have prepared in advance, you will save a lot of time. Sitting and having a coffee and socializing can set a poor example for the staff and volunteers. If you were to total up the combined amount of time spent over a period of a month, you'll be shocked to learn of how many nonproductive hours were lost because you were not focused and either had not made plans the night before or failed to stick to them. Remember – when at work – there's ALWAYS Lots To Do! Focus on the sales and everything else will take care of itself.

FIRST THINGS FIRST - AS EASY AS A,B,C!

Take care of your priority tasks first! The reward will be a sense of satisfaction and increased confidence that you are in control of the situation and of yourself. Then, if an interruption occurs, or problems requiring your attention happen, you are able to take care of them knowing that you have already dealt with your top-priority item. If you delay your high-priority item until the afternoon, chances are you will get off track and spend your time on less important work. Often business people feel trapped in a never-ending circle of other's demands or distractions, which could so readily be avoided by using time management techniques.

Give Yourself A Chance

So as to get to your high priority tasks, you will need to have some uninterrupted time. Don't answer calls for the first hour of each day, or get to work before opening time. It's amazing how much you can accomplish when focused and uninterrupted. You have to make it happen, otherwise others may not be aware of your needs and want some of your time for their needs.

Get The Lead Out!

Avoid procrastinating. Set dead lines, as well as priorities so you will be more inclined to complete the job in a timely manner.

If you are procrastinating starting a major project because it appears so big and you don't know where to begin, split the major project into manageable pieces.

An example may be taking inventory and assigning values to each item can seem like a huge effort. One day's approach can be to decide in advance how the items are to be grouped.

Another day, determine the time of day you will do the counting and how much you will accomplish at a time. Later you can discuss your plans with volunteers, for their input and arrange a time when the most help will be available.

Write It Down – Then Relax

Using some form of a calendar will help you keep track of things that need to be done at a specific time – for example a pick-up at a donor's home. When scheduling your workday, allow yourself some flexibility and time for things that are unexpected, as things don't always go according to plan.

Allow yourself enough time so that you work in a thoughtful, unhurried manner.

Having an up to date and efficient filing system preferably on a computer will enable you to find your files quickly. Paper is still inevitable, it seems. You'll need to keep copies of your important correspondence, and bookkeeping records. To try and keep paper to a minimum, ask yourself? How important is this to me or my business, why would I need to refer to this in the future?

Professional Time Managers strongly advise to keep your work desk uncluttered. It will allow you to focus on the task at hand, rather than feeling overwhelmed and distracted as soon as you see your messy desk.

Don't Be Afraid to Delegate – You Must!

As your company expands, you may need to increase the number of volunteers, and hire staff. You'll need to delegate some of your duties. Workers enjoy added responsibilities and authorities. Delegating activities builds staff morale.

Just Say No When You Need To

People will see how you are succeeding in business and may sometimes ask you to volunteer for community posts, taking time from your business day. Being aware of your daily workload you may have to say no - which is important to your time management.

Your bookkeeper is the backbone of your business.

Modern bookkeeping has been simplified enormously with the use of computerized programs.

Your professional accountant will still take care of your business's tax returns and all you need to do is learn to enter the pertinent information.

Spending even 5 – 10 minutes a day entering your days sales and expenses will assist your bookkeeper and especially your accountant greatly.

This will help you save more money, whatever bookkeeping software you may use.

With your accounting software, you could handle some bookkeeping tasks that you might otherwise outsource. That can save you money, especially if you don't have significant bookkeeping needs and if you have someone who can handle bookkeeping tasks in addition to other duties.

Garbage In, Garbage Out

It's important that you are entering the information into your software program accurately. An extra zero or two at the end of an amount can make a tremendous difference in the getting reliable results or not.

Bookkeeping programs can be tremendous money and time savers for your business There are lots of opportunities to learn how to use these programs properly and you'll need to be patient with yourself in the beginning. At first, its reassuring to have an experienced person look your work over and make sure you are doing it correctly so that your accountant will not have to spend much time looking for information that you can easily provide.

If you are just not interested in pursuing bookkeeping, or feel it is not in your best interest, don't worry about it. Find a reliable person who has experience entering the data and let them do it. For these duties, the bookkeeper will do the work at their home, on a contract basis, which saves you space and bother. You can phone or email the days transaction to the bookkeeper on a regular basis, so as to keep an up-to-the-minute current balance.

Keeping Safe Control Of Your Business

If your books are not kept up to date and carefully balanced, **your business is out of control** and will be like a ship running at night with no navigation equipment.

> **It's that important - to somehow always have an accurate bank balance and to know if you are making a profit on a regular basis.**

Forewarned is fore armed as the old saying goes. If you find out that you are losing money, you have the knowledge to change the situation and turn your business around, either by increasing sales or reducing expenses, or both.

Bookkeeping software programs can be used for much more than just a business's annual profit and losses. They also can:

- Generate payrolls, track and pay corporate tax and employer tax liabilities, print out employee W-2s and contractor Form 1099s, and track overdue bills.
- Link to online banking services and accounts, so that banking information is automatically incorporated into the software program.

One of the most important tasks of any bookkeeping system, whether manual or computerized is to provide you with an accurate, on the spot bank account balance. You must always be able to determine exactly the financial resources you have available and how much you can write a check for if you need to.

The rest of the information is important, but this is such a fundamental necessity that it needs to be emphasized.

What is it that you like doing? If you don't like it, get out of it, because you'll be lousy at it. You don't have to stay with a job for the rest of your life, because if you don't like it you'll never be successful in it.

Lee Iacocca
(Former) Chairman of Chrysler Corporation

Chapter 11

Staff Issues, Volunteer Appreciation

Employee Or Contractor?

Other than a trades person who you may call in for a specific job, very few people who work for your business will qualify as a contractor. If the Tax Department states that a worker should have been treated as an employee, you will have to pay the payroll taxes plus penalties and interest.

To be seen as an "independent contractor", the worker needs to fit the following:

- possess their own business cards
- proof of their independent status
- have their own business bank account
- have their own business license
- works for a number of other customers – not just for you
- Supplies their own tools, equipment for the job

REGULATION OF WAGES AND HOURS

Minimum Wages changes from time to time and can be found on the Internet or by contacting your local Labor standards office.

Usually you will attract a more reliable, long term worker by offering several dollars above the minimum wage.

Employers need to pay employees at time-and-a-half for any time worked over eight hours a day or over 40 hours a week. This is also subject to change from area to area.

SECURITY

Small merchandise, electronics and anything of value that can be easily concealed, will attract shoplifters, as well as paying customers. Shoplifting can be a problem at thrift stores.

Anti-shoplifting signs on the interior of the store, along with real or dummy closed circuit cameras can be a helpful deterrent. The most important protection against shoplifting will be the powers of observation, by you or your volunteers on duty.

An effective form of protection from burglary when the store is closed is a motion detection alarm.

There are many low cost alarm systems, which are monitored, so that if they are set off, the alarm monitoring station will notify you and the local police.

Train your volunteers to become watchful with some of the obvious signs of a shoplifter.

Would be shoplifters may often be anxious, looking around a lot to see if anyone is watching them. That alone makes them appear suspicious.

Sometimes they may spend an excessive amount of time in the same area – handling a product, or take it with them from one area to another.

You can instruct volunteers to observe these behaviors and let you know promptly if they witness any strong indications of shoplifting. It is a serious accusation to make toward a customer, so you must be confident before approaching a suspect.

Its good to have a clear sign near the checkout, requesting persons carrying shopping bags, briefcases, or backpacks, to leave them at the counter with you. If a visitor to the store doesn't notice the sign, or ignores it, its acceptable to just mention it to the visitor and maybe point to the sign, with a smile. Prevention is much easier to deal with than having to risk making a false accusation.

"Honesty" Always Is The Best Policy

Industry figures show that sales staff steals twice as much merchandise as outside thieves, including shoplifters. Chain clothing stores are extremely strict with the sales staff and have quite elaborate procedures to prevent theft from staff. To prevent this problem, all job applicants should be carefully screened and their references checked. A safe for locking up purses, bags, and cash (for later deposit in the bank) is also advisable. Access to any safe and keys to the facility should be restricted to the most trusted employees.

Be watchful about money and merchandise. Keep track of daily register shortages for each employee responsible for the cash drawer that day. If an employee is dipping into the till, you'll soon notice a pattern. Sometimes a large discount may be given to a person who is not entitled to it, but could be a friend of the cashier.

Also, in your daily and monthly cash register reports, keep an eye on "no sales" and total reductions. Too many of these on a certain register that the same employee is working on, may indicate a problem.

To learn what your security risks are and to get protection, contact local "Security Control Equipment and Systems" companies listed in your Yellow Pages. Also, your local police department will help you with ideas and suggestions to improve your store security.

If your New Years resolution is to give back to your community here's your chance!

We currently have volunteer openings. Discover treasures at Clothes and Collectibles. It's Xmas everyday. Help sell, price, sort, organize donated items. A gift of 4 hours/week supports the programs of the _____ Seniors' Network. Help a home bound senior with their grocery shopping by volunteering for our weekly shopping program. A 4 hr. shift per week ensures that someone is eating. Bring your professional skills to the "Manor" by providing weekly sessions – manicures, pedicures, massage therapy or other therapeutic art. Professional credentials must be provided. A gift of health. We also need hosts for our regular Classic TV and Documentary screening and discussion groups.

It's All Text, but From the Heart!

SAFETY AND HEALTH STANDARDS

State and Provincial authorities regulate working conditions, especially in regard to safety and health.

Federal and local laws require employers to provide employees with a workplace that is free of physically harmful agents as well as a reasonable temperature range to work in. It is the employer's responsibility to be fully aware and in compliance with these requirements, so as to meet the law, but more importantly protect volunteers or employers in your business.

According to OSHA, the most frequently repeated violations are unclearly marked or unmarked exits, locations of fire extinguishers or if they are not mounted properly and fall-dangerously piled boxes or containers in storerooms.

Safety inspectors can appear at the business unannounced at any time and without advance notice.

Violations of safety and health laws can result in severe severe fines, or even forced closure of the business until the standards are proved to have been met.

ADDING TO YOUR TEAM

Ask applicants pertinent questions, to see if they are looking for long term or if they are sure of what they are getting into – could work with other volunteers for an orientation. Ask what they would like to get out of the experience.

Volunteer appreciation dinners or parties can go a long way to creating long term happy volunteers. Some regular form of recognition for their help is essential.

Be sure to thank them for their efforts each time they come in to work.

Putting a Help Wanted or Volunteers Wanted sign in the window can be quite effective. Have some blank application forms handy, for the walk-in applicant to fill out.

You can do a short stand up interview while they are present, or give them a call later to set an appointment, after you have had time to review their application.

Interviewing Volunteers or Paid Applicants

You can save everybody time, by doing a short pre- interview chat by phone. Describing the position's duties and expectations can help clarify the opportunity. When the phone interview is done and you believe the applicant understands the job requirements, call them in for personal interviews.

If you are serious about the candidate after you have conducted the interview, check those references to verify their employment history.

Try to put the applicant at ease and to be comfortable. You can help break the ice by doing the talking first. Briefly go over the duties and tell them about your business, the positive signs it is showing, and where you expect it to head in the future. Showing your enthusiasm about the business will be infectious and the applicant will be encouraged to see the store as a going concern.

Volunteers Needed Donations Welcome!

During the interview, pay attention to the applicant's appearance and attitude. If a person seems shy or not very forthcoming, you can assume this person will be the same or more so with customers. A person who is more sociable and outgoing would be more friendly and hospitable towards people who come into your store. By being observant, you can read between the lines and can often learn more than from direct questions.

Let the interviewee talk freely. Listen to both what the person says and doesn't say.

For example, if a person talks about what a lousy boss he has now, and complains about what poor bosses he's had in the past, it's possible this person has trouble getting along with people, especially authority figures. If an applicant has gone from one job to another finding fault with each job, they may only last a short time with your business.

Direct the discussion into various channels to find out as much as possible about the person. If not already known, discuss past wages or salaries and expected compensation. Keep salaries in line with the competition—or better, if you can afford it.

It's good to make some notes either during the interview or soon after, as it's so easy to forget details when you are interviewing a number of potential volunteers / employees.

With proper planning and well thought out questions, hiring the right applicant can make a big difference to your business.

Don't jump to hiring a person because you like them – this is not enough reason to hire any staff. They may be friendly, but lack the experience and knowledge you need.

Choose mature staff that will be willing to learn about every aspect of the business. It's best to get people who enjoy being trained and gradually taking more responsibility, so if one person has to be away or is sick, you still have a knowledgeable person to rely on. Plus learning on the job does make it more interesting.

VOLUNTEER PROGRAMS

Besides considering what your volunteers want from their jobs and how you can achieve the goal of an efficient, happy and productive staff, you must recognize the legal framework within which all personnel policies operate

All successful business owners must recognize that fair wages, attractive fringe benefits, desirable working conditions, and concern for employees are important parts of building a dedicated and efficient staff. Such a staff will advance your business goals and, by word-of-mouth, create an image of your business as a good place to work. Even small things such things as free coffee or tea can be a benefit. A free lunch or take out food once in awhile can be a nice surprise. Remembering an employees or volunteer 's birthday with a cake can also get you some good mileage as being thoughtful.

Building Morale

Its very rewarding to the employee/volunteer to know that you respect their opinions and will sometimes use their ideas in the business. Also, to give them full credit for their input. They will feel valued and a feeling of cooperation will thrive and contribute to a positive group spirit.

A healthy employee morale and team spirit will make your days seem shorter and add to the enjoyment of the workday.

Some suggestions to help you achieve good morale at your business::

1.   Understand that other opinions may correct, and learn from them.

2.   Work on increasing your understanding of human psychology.

3. Let your staff know that you are interested in them, and welcome their ideas.

4. Be tolerant and respectful to all.

5. Encourage promotion from within the business. Consider this when hiring staff or engaging volunteers.

6. Provide an orientation when a new person joins your staff – advise them on safety and security matters. People need to feel secure at work.

7. Regard each of your staff as unique individuals, each with their own assets and liabilities.

8. Keep your people informed of any business matters that may affect them

9. Make an effort to keep jobs interesting and give opportunities for learning..

10. Good communications with the staff is important, to prevent gossip and worries from mounting.

11. Good work deserves recognition - Volunteer of the Month – gets a privileged parking spot, etc.

12. Rather than simple criticism, make the situation into a learning situation for the employee/ volunteer. Be discreet, speak to him/her in private

STAFF POSITIONS

In your thrift store business, you will have the standard retail sales group of owner, (manager,) sales clerk and / or volunteers.

Each has their own duties and responsibilities.

MANAGER — THAT'S YOU SIR (OR MA'M)!

The manager has direct responsibility for the profitability of the store.

The manager should have retail sales background and preferably some experience in supervising others. A sense of maturity is important in the manager, if he/ she is to be respected by his/her staff. Probably you won't interview previous thrift store people, but if you do, be aware that the applicant will need to be flexible and not want to do everything the same as in their previous position. They need to be able to adapt to your ideas and practices.

You will usually be the Manager as well as the owner, until your business has the volume of sales

that it needs to hire another paid person.

Sometimes if you have a volunteer who is particularly keen, you can approach them about a paid part time manager's position. They may not want the responsibility, but it would be to your advantage to hire a person familiar with the thrift store industry – or a related type of business like a dollar store, consignment business, or some sort of clothing retail management experience.

The manager's duties include responsibility for supervising store operations and providing quick and courteous service to all customers by determining their needs. They will train associates on product knowledge and selling skills. He/she looks after scheduling and the prioritizing of work of associates and ensures satisfactory completion of all tasks.

The manager is responsible for the overall financial performance of the store including sales, expense control, and meeting of profit goals. They ensuring that new merchandise gets to the sales floor as required and that all possible loss prevention policies are followed.

Don't be afraid to offer a small piece of the action— perhaps 1 to 2 percent of the net as an incentive.

SALES ASSISTANTS

Any staff or volunteer who has contact with the customers needs to be friendly, polite and positive. You'll want your staff to have a reasonable knowledge of your sponsoring charity – enough to at least know how to direct enquiries about the organization.

Take the time to regularly offer some information about the charity and have pamphlets available for interested visitors.

Sales clerks need to be very familiar with the locations of merchandise, so that when asked by a customer, the sales clerk can readily tell them or show them where to find it. They generally need to be familiar with the inventory and have a knowledge of whether your store has the requested product.

NEWSPAPER AD FOR VOLUNTEERS AND DONATIONS

Sometimes you will want to put a small display advertisement in your local weekly paper soliciting donations – that is a good time to solicit for volunteers as well. You can mention the charity you donate to at the same time.

Every city or community has a central volunteer coordinator. Place newspaper ads to find sales clerks, full- or part-time. Also consider placing notices on the bulletin boards of local colleges for an abundance of part-timers. Regardless of where you get the part-time help, have all applicants fill out personnel forms so you can check references. Occasionally you'll find a part-timer who's worked in a clothing or other related type of store.

Salaries for full-time salespersons vary with the cost of living and prevailing wage in your area.

Involving Your Volunteers

Many new business owners become married to their businesses, never enjoying a few days off or taking a vacation because they do not trust the work to someone else. Sometimes, the business may be restricted from growing because of a lack of staff/ volunteers.

There are a lot of people who enjoy volunteering – all you have to do is invite them to help, and treat them well.

Depending on the size of the community the store is in - for example a small rural city, your business has a somewhat limited supply of applicants.

But rest assured, there are wonderful, intelligent people in unlimited numbers who enjoy volunteering for a community based fundraiser like your thrift store business.

Never stop selling the qualities and benefits of your thrift store. A positive attitude in the media and in person goes a long way towards attracting positive people.

Hiring friends or family can lead to problems down the road, even though it starts out with good intentions. If they don't work out and you have to let them go, you lose both an employee and a good relationship. It can get messy very quickly.

Try to be realistic in your expectations of an employee. They will never be perfect – any more than you or I will, but as long as they are willing to learn from you exactly what you expect, and you have patience, you will both be successful. On the other hand, a person that ignores your training and continues to make errors must be corrected and disciplined. You will be making a significant investment in time and earnings for each employee, so try to retain them. Training new employees can be expensive and time consuming.

The resentment that criticism engenders can   demoralize employees, family members and   friends, and still not correct the situation that   has been condemned.

Dale Carnegie
Famous Author

VOLUNTEER SERVICES APPLICATION

This information is CONFIDENTIAL Volunteer!

Date Received in Office: _____

PERSONAL INFORMATION

Please Print:

Name: _____

      First   Middle   Last

Address: _____

City: _____

State/Province: _____

Zip/Postal Code: _____

Home Phone _____

Work Phone _____

Email: _____

Cell/Pager: _____

EMERGENCY INFORMATION

Name _____

Emergency Phone: _____

EMPLOYMENT/LANGUAGE/EDUCATION

Are you currently employed? Yes _____ No _____

Current or previous work experience _____

_____

_____

_____

_____

Do you have a Drivers License? Yes _____ No _____
Class _____

Do you have: Car___ Truck ___ SUV ____ Van ____

EDUCATION   (Please Check)

Secondary _____Post-secondary _____

Degree/Diplomas obtained _____

First Language: _____

Understand ____Read____Speak ____Write ____

Second Language: _____

Understand ____Read____Speak ____Write ____

American Sign Language for the Deaf? Yes__No __

REASONS FOR VOLUNTEERING: _____

_____

_____

How did you hear about us?

Volunteer Centre ____Newspaper____Brochure____
Friend/Family ____Internet/Website ____ TV ____
Personal ____College/University ____Events ____

Other _____

PLEASE INDICATE YOUR PREFERENCES BELOW

Sales____Cashier ____ Sorter ____

Customer Pick up ____Housekeeping ____

Sewing ____ Steaming of clothing____

Please check personal skills that you would be
interested in sharing with us.

Sales____Customer Service ____Receiving ____

Tidying and Displays____Fluff and Fold____

Computer/Internet____Accounting ____

Business/Marketing ____Media ____

Public Relations ____

Please list any additional skills/interests that you might like to contribute while volunteering at Thrift Store:

_____

_____

_____

_____

AVAILABILITY & COMMITMENT
FOR ALL YOUR INTEREST AREAS

Thrift Store Volunteers are asked to seriously consider a commitment of four hours per week for six months. Please circle the day/s you would like to come in. We will do our best to oblige you.

M, T, W, T, F, S

Morning_____Afternoon _____

AREAS OF INTEREST

My name may be made available for volunteer recognition purposes and activities Yes____No____

I have read and understand the above information and give my consent which is provided voluntarily.

Print Name: _____

Signature: _____

Date: _____

REFERENCES

For a volunteer position please list two contact references below. Please note that it is not necessary to complete and forward any additional reference forms. Please list other than friends.

Please Print:

1. Name: _____

Relationship to you _____

Address: _____

City: _____

Zip/Postal Code: _____

Telephone: _____

2. Name: _____

Relationship to you _____

Address: _____

City: _____

Zip/Postal Code: _____

Telephone: _____

*You have a task to perform and
are vitally interested in it, excited
and challenged by it, then you will
exert maximum energy. But in
the excitement, the pain of fatigue
dissipates, and the exuberance of what
you hope to achieve overcomes the
weariness.*

Jimmy Carter
Former President of USA

CHAPTER 12

SALES AND MARKETING —
WHERE YOU MAKE YOUR MONEY!

THE PURPOSE OF ADVERTISING

Advertising is a direct way to reach both current and prospective customers which enables you to:

Convince customers and clients that your Thrift Store's many bargains are the best. It's like a form of education as well as sales.

Advertisements That Really Work for Your Business

- They are simple and easily understood.
- They are truthful.
- They are informative
- They are sincere.
- They tell who, what, when, where, why and how.

THRIFT SHOP *Clothing Etc.*

SUMMER SALE
UP TO 50% OFF
Friday, July 20th &
Saturday, July 21st

A Good Clearance Offer - To Save More

THE 4 R's –
REDUCE, REUSE, RECYCLE, AND RECOVER

Most of our garbage is sent to landfills, dumps or municipal incinerators. But with more and more people producing more and more waste, landfills are filling up faster than we can find new sites for them. And landfills create new types of waste. As garbage decomposes, moisture filters through it producing a toxic liquid known as leachate. Modern landfills are designed to reduce the amount of moisture that reaches the garbage, and many have a system to collect and treat the leachate.

Garbage gone but not forgotten!

Decomposing garbage also produces two greenhouses gases: carbon dioxide and methane, an invisible, odorless, and highly flammable gas. At some big landfill sites, methane is now being collected and burned to produce energy.

Water and oxygen are required to break down garbage. But water and oxygen are in short supply deep in a landfill, so decomposition takes place very slowly.

In fact, when researchers cored down into a landfill in the United States, they discovered newspapers over 30 years old still in readable condition!

Incinerations are sometimes used to burn solid waste under controlled condition. They reduce the stress on landfills, but they create other environmental problems. The ashes must be disposed of, either at a landfill, or, if they are toxic, at a hazardous waste facility. Burning garbage also produces acid gases, carbon dioxide and toxic chemicals that must be treated with expensive air pollution control equipment to avoid contributing to acid rain, ozone depletion and air pollution.

Recycling is just one way to reduce wastes. To be really effective, we have to incorporate the 4Rs Reduce, Reuse, Recycle and Recover into our daily routine.

Reducing the amount of waste we produce is by far the most effective way to battle the flow of garbage into the landfill. Packaging makes up about half our garbage by volume, one-third by weight.

* When you shop, try to find products that have little or no packaging.

WHAT WE CANNOT REDUCE WE CAN TRY TO REUSE

Materials and packaging that cannot be reused can be recycled at home, work and school. Everyone can contribute to recycling by purchasing recycled and recyclable products at , for example, Thrift Stores!

Finally, Recover energy from wastes that cannot be used for something else. This fourth R is difficult to put into practice by individuals, and is geared more toward industry.

Recycled

This symbol means that the product is made from material that has been used before. If there is no qualifying statement (ex. "60% post consumer recycled content") then symbol means the product is 100% recycled.

Recyclable

Recyclable only means that a material or product can be recycled. It does not necessarily contain recycled material.

YOUR GRAND OPENING IS A MEDIA EVENT!
CREATE A TRAFFIC JAM!

When you open your business, take a picture of your staff and the building. Have the picture blown up to an 8 X 10 glossy black white print. Then write a brief story about your business.

Let your prospective customers know you exist. This will result in your advertising costs being higher the first year of operation.

Advertising has a cumulative effect. Response is slow at first but increases with time; sporadic splurges rarely pay off.

It is a much better effect to advertise regularly and continuously on a small scale than to place large advertisements infrequently.

Send this to the city editor of your newspaper with the heading, "For Release on X Date." Or, if you are running a grand opening ad, give the release to the ad salesperson, who will make certain it gets into the paper.

- NEW LOOK TO AN OLD BUSINESS!

- GARAGE SALES DECLARED OBSOLETE!

You may follow the same process with your local radio and TV stations. Television and radio use much less news of this type than newspapers, but when they have a slow news day, you may find yourself getting some free publicity.

Handle your Grand Opening in a professional style. But don't make the mistake of classing yourself out of business. You still want to attract bargain hunters; they will give you some of your best sources of income.

Advertising Tips

One of the many customers you will have to sell clothing, furniture and household effects to are theatre groups, high school acting classes. You may want to put a small ad in the program for the play or concert, to keep your name in front of the public and help build goodwill.

Near Halloween – advertise for public to find their costumes at your store.

Make sure your customers know about all the good things you do – for example how much you donated to your sponsoring charity over the last three months, how you helped out a homeless shelter.

You can run relevant ads for your charity, to help raise awareness, with mention of your store in it.

You are going to need some type of sales promotion. Effective advertising will greatly increase your business success. Customers need to know you are open on a continuing basis. Approximately 20 per cent of the population moves every year, so there is a steady stream of potential donors and customers to be kept informed of your business.

Especially when starting the business, make your advertising is donein such a way as to be measured.

Collection bins are sometimes used so people can drop off donations any time. If you do this it's an advertising opportunity, by putting your store name, phone number and address. This type of bin should be placed in a well lit area, with good visibility from the street, to avoid vandalism or being used for junk. Often local dry cleaners will put some form of container for the public to put their used clothing in.

Tracking Your Ads – Finding Out What Works

Keep track of when your advertising appears to the public and any changes in sales or donations in the week or so following.

This will give you some idea of how your ad is performing. Many variables can be considered to influence the public's response, such as contents of the ad, the economy, weather conditions, time of year, and other such factors will affect any advertising program. Even if you don't get big results at first, some people will remember your business and visit you at another time.

Promotions Increase Sales

Sales promotion will:

- attract new consumers and hold present ones,
- enable you to compete with other businesses

You can use any promotions that much larger businesses do – just on a smaller scale!

Use of any or all of the following:

- advertising,
- publicity,
- public relations activities,
- special "sales" (clearances, close-outs, Back to School, etc.),
- contests, and
- window displays or
- focusing on a specific type of product such as electronics, kitchen table sets and so on.

Aggressively be on the lookout for occasions to give your thrift store broad and regular exposure .

This is How To Get Noticed!

CREATE SOME EXCITEMENT!

A popular contest is to hold a raffle for a gift certificate. You can draw attention by using window banners, in-store signs, or during any special sales you run from time to time. Customers fill out a free entry blank with name, address, and phone number, then put them into a box. Indicate when the draw will be, and invite some local newspaper reporters to report the drawing.

You can always arrange to take the photo yourself and publish it as an ad in your paper as well. Winners receive gift certificates to your store in the dollar amount as advertised. Mention on the certificates that they are good for merchandise only – no refunds or cash value.

INCENTIVES – MAKE THEM AN OFFER: THEY CAN'T REFUSE!

Things to consider when planning:

What And When To Promote:

Look at what type of merchandise will produce the best profits along with the season. Eg. Sleds, winter clothing in the Fall, Winter.

Furniture and larger items do have a higher price range, therefore a larger profit opportunity.

Quantities and types of donations will also influence what you want to move out of the store. If for example, the store is getting a lot of dishes, and they are building up, that would be a good opportunity to reduce their level to normal.

Promoting does not always have to mean a price reduction. By increasing the public's awareness of your store and of the benefits of shopping there along with focusing on certain products you can help increase sales. It probably has not occurred to many consumers that they can purchase a baby carriage or a new to them bicycle at your thrift store for a fraction of the new price.

Everybody Loves A Good Clearance Sale!

You will find that as donations increase, some merchandise accumulates over time. Depending on the previously mentioned considerations, you can use newspaper ads to clear out these goods.

Making your sale over a period of a Thursday, Friday and Saturday can bring the best sales. That is when most large stores have their sales, since it is when the public likes to shop. Being aware of the payroll days for major employers can also increase your sales substantially, if you can reach those people when they have money to spend.

In-store advertising, window banners or including a small flyer with a customer's purchase are proven methods of reaching your target market.

A little discount coupon for a percentage discount off their next purchase can keep your customers returning.

Even a small percentage Discount or money amount will increase sales.

Frequency Of Price Reductions

Be aware of how often you are offering lower than usual prices on your merchandise. If it becomes too regular, customers will put off their purchases until the next sale. Increasing awareness of your store and of the benefits of shopping there will be more rewarding to you in the long run.

DISPLAYS- OUTDOOR AND WINDOW

Display windows or outdoor displays of things like lawn mowers, or baby carriages may be used as valuable advertising space in front of the store, that impresses passing traffic and gets their attention.

Keep your windows working for you and change the items in it frequently. Its really no-cost advertising, if you make good use of it. Simply using the space for storage gives an impression of clutter and disarray. Some thrift store owners have even put a sign in the window saying when the goods displayed will be available for sale, since the pieces sell so quickly, that they did not have the time to be replacing the window displays constantly.

**A nice problem! And one that can
be dealt with in many ways.**

EXPRESS YOUR CREATIVITY AND SELL MORE!

When possible, create interesting displays that will
make people want to look inside. A sense of humor or
an unexpected arrangement can be very helpful and
creative. It also shows the public that your store is
busy and lively, not a dusty quiet place that could be
boring.

You have a great opportunity to make your
business thrive, by advertising promoting and being

Attractive Window Display Is Inviting

watchful for chances to increase the community's awareness of the many benefits of shopping with you.

Merchandising Your Goods So They Look Enticing

DON'T cram every square foot of your selling space with merchandise. With such a variety of goods, you need to have as much of your merchandise on display for customer to browse through. You can have circular and rectangular racks, depending on the type of equipment you can pick up.

Straight, double sided racks with a shelf above the middle are very useful for displaying ornaments, dishes and such.

Here and there you may want a mannequin. The thing to keep in mind is that the right fixtures will allow you to keep the merchandise on display for the shoppers.

Location Matters In Marketing

Your advertising budget will be dependent on your store's location. For example, if you are located in a mall that does a lot of advertising or have a lot of major traffic producing businesses nearby you'll probably have enough walk-ins from the time you open without much advertising.

The higher rent in a mall or central business area will help generate more sales than quieter areas.

If you think you are beaten, you are If
you think you dare not, you don't If
you like to win but you think you can't
It's almost certain you won't

Napoleon Hill
Think and Grow Rich

Chapter 13

Advanced Marketing

Free Media Exposure – Better Than Paid Advertising

You can get free media exposure which will support your personal credibility and increase public awareness of you as a reliable, conscientious member of the business community.

Being a thrift store operator appeals to a broad audience – whether it be the environmentally aware sector, charitable organizations or bargain hunters. You can approach a newspaper, and find out who to speak with, to set up an interview. Or you can issue a news release.

The important issue here is to offer a unique view of your operation – an interesting angle that readers would find fresh and different. Keep it upbeat and positive, so the readers will have a good impression of you and what you are doing. It's often overlooked how important re-using goods is to the environment. It's an important message to get out – and one that will benefit you and your business.

Explain in your conversation, why you believe this story will be of interest to the readers, without criticizing or being negative in any way.

RADIO AND TELEVISION TALK SHOWS

Sometimes a Public Service radio or television talk show will also be interested in your topics. A friendly, relaxed approach is more acceptable to them than a person who is very nervous or unable to sit still for a few minutes. You can even write out the questions for the interviewer to ask you as well as your introduction for their use. The more prepared you are, the less resistance you will encounter, and the more welcomes you will get.

Once you have found the contact person, briefly sell him or her on the benefits to the listeners when you are being interviewed on the program. If possible, try to have a representative from your sponsoring charity as well. The organization will appreciate your efforts to raise awareness of their charity.

**The publicity will be more
valuable than spending a fortune
on advertising.**

Letters To The Editor

It's usually easy to have your letter published in the
"letters to the editor" section of a local newspaper.
Write about a subject that is current and related
somehow to your business, as well as being positive
and courteous. Mention in the letter that you are
a thrift store owner and have expertise and many
concerns in the recycling area. You could make an
observation about the high quality of donations your
store receives, as a reflection of the importance of
recycling.

Have Articles Written About You – You ARE Doing Important Work!

For example, every time you make a donation to your
sponsoring charity, or are expanding the store, or any
other community related action it all has news value.

With occasional press releases and having
some of them published, you will be regarded as an
authority in your area. The media may look to you
for a quote for an article on the topic. It all depends
on how you present yourself and your business –
enthusiasm counts, as does a good knowledge of your
subject matter.

For example, "look at how this form of recycling
benefits the environment, donors and buyers." The

fact that you are being written about (even if you wrote much of the article for the reporter) adds a lot of credibility to your business and to you personally.

ENCOURAGE YOUR LOCAL NEWSPAPER EDITOR TO SELL FOR YOU

A newspaper editor's major problem is filling the paper with newsworthy items. Local newspapers are most interested in local news, and that's what you are as a local business owner.

When you start a new business, when you have a contest promotion, when you do something charitable, when something unusual happens to you, your business, or your employees, these are newsworthy events and worth letting the media know about. Why is publicity so important, and what will it do that advertising won't? In general, a news story or magazine article takes more time to read than an ad. The more time a reader spends with your story, the more likely he is to remember you.

You can have news releases and feature stories published without any cost to you.

An article in a respected newspaper or magazine will only be approved if the editor deems it of general interest. By being seen as an article in a newspaper rather than an ad, it adds credibility to your story that you can't buy. Articles that are published can be framed and put on exhibit in the store. How to impress your friends and visitors! Make a photocopy of the article first, so it doesn't go yellow with age!

When getting ready to submit an article or news release, call the newspaper or ask for the City Desk. They will guide you to the person to speak to. It's all much easier than most people would expect it to be.

Become Media Wise And
Keep Your Sponsor Charity Involved

Involving your charity sponsor can be very effective for increasing the charity's profile, increasing understanding of what they are doing to help their cause, and increase awareness of your thrift store and your donations to the charity.

Published photos of passing a giant check to the executive director of your charity can be a great way to give you both publicity. It's important for the public to see that you are being supportive to a good cause.

Keep alert to anything that can give you publicity. The media may accept not everything, but whatever is accepted will be a form of free advertising for you. Be sure to reprint all your publicity stories and news releases. Use them as highly credible advertising handouts and mailers. Your charity sponsor will be appreciative of raising public awareness of them.

DESIGNING AN EFFECTIVE AD - BY YOURSELF!

No matter what form of advertising you choose
for your thrift store, all good advertising has basic
requirements to ensure its effectiveness. Always be
sure to include the name of your store prominently
as well as address, hours of operation, volunteers
needed, donations needed - be specific if you need to,
i.e. warm coats.

Ad sales people will help you design your ad and
say what you want to say. Usually, thrift stores ads
just say " Donations Needed, Volunteers welcome.
In support of - - - - charity – but can also offer
free pickup, tax receipts and mention how they are
benefiting charity!

I saw one ad recently that proclaimed " We aim
to keep the word "Thrift" in thrift store shopping"

Next, you have to design an appeal—that is,
something that will benefit the target audience—and
incorporate it into ad copy. Here are some guidelines
that, if followed, will help you create strong, response-
getting ads:

Create a sense of immediacy. Because response
diminishes over time, advertising relies on getting
people to act immediately.

Most people like to be led — particularly when in unfamiliar territory. Tell your audience what response you want. At different points throughout the ad, and especially at the conclusion, ask for a physical response:

- "Act quickly,"
- "Limited time offer,"
- "Call now," etc.

You may want to stress to your consumers that your entire inventory changes every 60 days: this will give them the fear of "missing out" on a great deal and increase the excitement of finding that "perfect bargain."

SPREADING YOUR MESSAGE, AND REINFORCING IT WITH REPETITION

Advertising regularly is important to build consumer awareness and get the message comprehended and noticed.

Because people are barraged with advertising messages from every direction, you need to compete with all the other businesses for the public's attention.

This doesn't mean you have to use full-page ads, but even a 2inch by 2 inch on a weekly basis will get noticed.

Persistence is what will help you to win the struggle for the public attention. The smaller ads run on a regular basis will get you more sales than a one time big splash with a full page ad.

We have seen the strongest results using bi-weeklies or weeklies. They cover a smaller area and have less distribution, but it is more focused and their rates are lower. If you decide to try running an ad in a monthly, commit to keeping it in that publication for six consecutive months.

KEEP REPEATING YOUR SALES BENEFITS AND STORE ADDRESS

Make it clear and easy for donors and customers to find you. You can keep telling the same story about your message in each of the ads, keeping it fresh and interesting by using a slightly new slant each time.

Repetition increases the believability of the ad and will increase sales every time someone hears or reads. That's why major businesses repeat their commercials and written ads so much.

Even if the repetition seems boring to you, when writing the ad copy, it won't be to the reader so you can repeat, repeat and repeat.

"Sell the sizzle, not the steak." This means sell the benefits not just your lightly used goods or your thrift store. Telling the world about the many positive features of the things you have for sale is great. The customers need to understand how your business works. Try to always be totally clear how your customers or your donors will directly benefit, the reader may miss the point you are making. To convince your potential customers, you must SELL the goods by describing them in colorful terms, using powerful terms. It doesn't have to be fancy or misleading, but presented in a positive manner that makes it appealing and gives a sense of urgency. By writing "This price is valid for a limited time only" readers will make a point of getting to your store as early as they can, to snatch up the bargain.

Pretend that you are writing an ad directed to a young teenager, so that everyone can understand your message.

TIP – being involved as a licensee with an organization whose purpose you strongly support can make a big difference in how easy it is for you to sell the good work they do. Sometimes thrift store operators have chosen a charity that they or a family member has had personal experience with. It could be a child you knew who had special needs, or a relative who suffered from an illness that a cure has still not been found for.

Evaluate Existing Ads – They Cost You

Collect all kinds of ads and study them. Learn what you like or don't like about them. You can use their ideas if the ad is effective. Don't try to re-invent the wheel, desperately trying to create everything new because you want to be different.

Certainly it is essential to put your own imagination to use, but learn to what really works – for similar size businesses that are successful with their advertising.

Getting The Most For Your Advertising Dollar

For print ads, you can normally get some sage advice from the salesperson about content, appearance and different offers that they may have seen be very successful.

Other ways to 'get noticed' in a print ad - one is to make an ad with some of "white space" or even reverse printing – where the background is dark and the print is a contrasting light color if you're advertising in newspapers, Or maybe a heavy box around the text if you're advertising in the Yellow Pages. These kinds of ads stand out from the others because of the rows of similar looking ads used.

Anything that looks different will catch the reader's eye.

Shape And Size Of Your Ad

The design of the ad is important, but so is the border or outline that it is in. An unusual ad size from standard formats will attract attention. Newspapers do have established sizes and shapes, but they want your business and may well be cooperative with your requests. It is in their interest to see you succeed, so you can spend more money with them. Don't allow a sales representative to rush you or discourage you from being creative. Most sales reps would not do that – but they do get paid a commission on their sales commission, so they need to keep selling. That's not your problem, so don't let it become a limitation to you.

Neighborhoods And Customers' Habits Change

As a thrift Storeowner, you need to understand the trends occurring in the market and in your customer's lives.

A good example is the current amount of publicity being given to global warming, its causes and consequences.

The public's awareness of the environment has been raised as never before. Buying lightly used products instead of brand new ones saves a lot of polluting and waste. Many of us do not realize how beneficial it is to shop at a thrift store when possible.

The effects on us individually as a consumer is significant, cost wise, but it also helps the planet.

Test how effective your advertisements are by keeping track of changes and the results in the changes. Write down the date of publication, then you can see any noticeable differences in daily sales shortly after the ad changes..

1. Try running the same ad in two different publications with an identifying mark or number on each.

    Ask the customer to bring the ad into the store to receive a special price or discount. See how many ads come in from each source.

    Don't be surprised if there are not a lot of ads brought in. It will depend a lot on how good the offer is! People will not go to the bother of cutting out an ad, unless they perceive it to be of significant importance.

    This method can also be used when seeking donations or volunteers. These subjects are just as measurable – they may not cut out the ad and bring it in, but it's a strong learning curve for you to ask the customer if they saw your ad and where.

2. Try stopping an ad for a few weeks and see if
    it makes any difference in sales. Results can
    also vary according to how established you are
    in the community.

HOW MUCH IS ENOUGH FOR AN AD BUDGET?

This will depend on your volume of sales. If the
business is just starting out or even in the first year
spending will likely need to be higher – perhaps
up to 10% of expected gross sales – if you are able
to determine what is working best for you. In the
beginning, you may have a lot of advertising sales
people trying to sell you everything from embossed
pens, key chains, to aircraft advertising in the sky!
Stick with the relatively small print ads in your weekly
newspaper. Don't allow yourself to get sidetracked or
convinced to splurge on expenses for unpredictable
results. Thrift stores average their ad budgets at 2 to
5 percent of their projected gross sales. If you are on
a busy street, with good walk in traffic, you may have
little need to advertise.

Since your thrift store draws its customers mainly
from the local community. In fact, the newspaper ad
may prove to be your most effective means of reaching
those who can use your products. A small display
ad in the free weekly paper is not expensive and will
expose your clothing, furniture and other goods and

services you provide to a great amount of potential customers.

In a suburbs area, shopper's papers are effective. As well you ad will be noticed more where there is less competition.

You may increase sales with classified display ads. They cost much less than display ads and may be located where your customers are looking – for a sofa or other furniture.

Try a small display ad or coupon in a local consumer newspapers, or "green sheets". These papers are targeted to a local neighborhood or suburb, and can be effective for reaching potential customers in that area.

THE YELLOW PAGES

The Yellow Pages are a year round source of information for users. Some companies may have photos and range in size from simple one-line listings to full-page spreads. The Yellow Pages is organized into specific categories according to types of businesses. Read through the ones pertaining to your business and be careful to choose the most appropriate one so people looking for your type of store will easily find you. It is usually worthwhile to have a least a simple line in any of the categories that people may look under. For example, you can have your main small ad under Thrift Stores. Be careful to meet the deadlines the Yellow Pages specifies for sending in your ad(s). Missing them can mean going a whole year without advertising in this important medium. (Display advertising in this category can be quite costly. It is an effective medium, for the whole year, and you will benefit from a simple line listing in several categories, rather than a display size.)

COMMUNITY INVOLVEMENT

Join local service groups where you can get your message out, whether it's a Toastmaster group, Rotary clubs, Chamber of Commerce – they are all enjoyable and do lots of good work in the community. Many of the members of these groups are also in business and welcome the chance to network with others The other members will tend to direct their business to your store, and influence their friends and family to do the same. No expense involved – a win-win situation for all!

Consumers may not realize that they can buy good used goods at a thrift shop and help reduce pollution until they read your ad. They may not even be aware that your store exists.

WEB SITE

When starting out, try to keep your website fairly simple. Use an easy to read font like Arial or New

Courier. Black colored print on a contrasting background is a going to be problem free.

The most common browsers are Microsoft Internet Explorer and/or Mozilla Firefox. Your web site should accommodate them both.

How often you should change your website's design is about the same as how often you should change the posters or signs in your store window – don't let either go stale. Updates on products, news about 'specials' or promotions you wish to focus on are important to keep the look current. Visiting your web site and seeing "old news" gives the impression that nobody is paying attention to the business or that nobody cares about it. Make your web site and your windows work for you. Including your web address in all ads, business cards or even on your answering service is a good policy.

Internet Advertising – on your local business and service associations website – don't have to have a web page, but do need to be found on the web. Yellow pages may give that choice. Check it out for effectiveness.

http://www.budgetcitythriftstore.com   (sample of a thrift store web site)

Create Your Own Web Page In Seconds, Gratis!

This has got to be the easiest and fastest way to create your own web page FREE and even have it hosted without charge. It seems to be a Google,com trial, so may not be free for long. http://pages.google.com/

Keeping The Website Interesting

On a thrift store business websites you have a great chance to promote your policies and approach to environmental issues. With so much rightful concern about global warming and things we can all do to reduce waste and pollution, this is a time to make a strong case for your thrift stores contributions to recycling and reusing good used products. There is next to no shipping involved with the products you are selling, resulting in no polluting of the air.

Once you start working on your site, you will be flooded with ideas and concepts you want to try out. Details of new products or services, hours and days of operation, pick up days for larger items and pointing out some of the pleasures of shopping at your store are all useful to the site visitor. You can even have a sign up feature for a newsletter or other news you can generate that would benefit the bargain hunter. Having photos and first names of some of your happy customers with testimonials can certainly add credibility to your image.

Designing An Effective Web Page

You will usually need a page or two at the most, as the Web visitor's attention span is not long.

Mentioning your latest donations is much easier to read and comprehend than a long tiresome list of products. You could mention that new items are always coming in to your store, so its in the customers best interest to visit regularly if they want to choose from the best variety.

A photo of your store front on a sunny day or even the interior can add a lot of interest. Usually these photos can be scanned onto the web site easily at home.

Make your "landing page" the first page - strong and bold. Have contrasting colors, some photos and short, punchy headlines. There many templates available free on the Internet, or the web host usually has a dozen or so templates available to you when you sign up for a web site with them.

You can design the template to look professional, even if you have little experience.

Try it yourself first before paying an expert.

Keep it looking uncluttered. Think of it like a newspaper or magazine ad. Allow for some white space, so that where you insert text or other materials, it grabs the viewer's attention.

Finding Help

If you do decide to get some professional help, do a search in the yellow pages of your phone book and on the internet. The designers do not need to be in your area. You can choose from a huge number of companies on the Internet. Often they are quite negotiable, so don't be afraid to ask for a better price or tell them how much you are prepared to spend.

You will encounter many distractions and many temptations to put your goal aside: The security of a job, a wife who wants kids, whatever. But if you hang in there, always following your vision, I have no doubt you will succeed.

Larry Flynt
Founder of Hustler magazine

A Sample Business Plan

Business Description

_____Thrift store is a new retail business venture that will begin operations on (date,) The business is a thrift store selling donated clothing, small house wares, books, jewelry, electronics, games, etc. It will serve the city of_____and the surrounding area. Our goals:

- to operate a for profit thrift store, and
- to be supportive of and donate ___% of gross sales to (charity) fund, on an ongoing basis.

Objectives

The primary objective of the company is to attain and maintain a position as the major source of good, used products for sale in the area, to be able to contribute significant funds to (charity)

Targets And Check List

Start accepting donations by _____

Obtain Lease by _____

Obtain Business License by _____

Required renovations on retail space by _____

Interview and schedule 6 volunteers by _____

Sort merchandise and hang up clothing by _____

Sort hardware and other donations and put out
stock by _____

Open the doors   (Soft opening) by _____

Grand Opening event by _____

Achieve $ in sales by_____

Achieve $ in sales by   _____

Interview and schedule additional volunteers
by   _____

Achieve $ in sales for the fiscal year _____

Purchase or lease a truck for donation pick _____

Hire a part time employee (date)_____

MARKETING OPPORTUNITIES

All indications are that the market for thrift stores continues to grow rapidly as awareness increases of the bargains contained in them. Word of mouth from shoppers who find prices in regular retail stores to be burdensome will continue to cause thrift shop sales to grow steadily in the foreseeable future. Growth estimates for the next three years range from 20% to 30%.per year.

With the threat of global warming ever becoming more of a reality, the benefits of recycling and re-using become more apparent. As well the for profit thrift store will be an affordable source of consumer products for persons who may be conscientious about spending their money wisely and in a manner benefiting the local community as well as themselves. Giving support to a cause they support, is an additional satisfaction.

COMPETITIVE ADVANTAGES

With no other retail outlet dedicated primarily to used goods in any direction, A Thrift Store will be in an excellent position to capture a large portion of the used items sales in the greater city area. We believe that there is a need for a Thrift Store and are poised to fill that need. As well, our Thrift Store will be donating substantial funds to (charity).

MARKETING STRATEGY

Our major target market is the greater (city) area
. There is very strong support for (charity), which
will show itself in support of the thrift store, with
donations and purchases. Families, and persons with
limited incomes are also a major target market as are
retirees.

Used items for sale will reflect the make up of
the community and their interests. In addition to low
priced men's and women's clothing , shoes and some
furniture, we will also stock household items, and a
wide range of good used products as they are donated.

CONFIDENTIALITY AND RECOGNITION OF RISKS

Confidentiality Clause

The information included in this business
plan is strictly confidential and is provided on the
understanding that it will not be disclosed to third
parties without the expressed written consent of

Recognition Of Risk

This business plan represents management's
best estimate of the future potential of our business
venture. All major risks cannot be accurately

predicted or otherwise avoided. Realistically, all business plans are bound to have some omissions or unintended errors..

Vision And Mission Statement

_____Thrift Store will become the premier source of good used retail products for (city) and surrounding communities Our goal is to provide customers with a wide variety of choices ; to promote recycling and support of_____ Charity in the community.

Objectives

Our primary objectives over the next year are:

- Obtain financing, negotiate a low cost lease in a semi-industrial or affordable retail area.
- Secure a licensing agreement with registered charity_____
- Obtain a term loan of $_____ in order to acquire fixtures for the store.
- Gain a market share of 20% of all thrift store items sold by the end of the first year of operations.
- Attain and maintain a position as the leading thrift store in the area.

Industry Overview

Market Research

To analyze the market potential of a thrift store in the area, we collected information from a number of sources.

We conducted a survey of residents in the (neighborhood, city) area, typically by stopping passers by on the street and asking them a few questions. The survey results were used to prepare customer profiles and gauge the acceptability of a thrift store in their area. There was a lot of enthusiasm and goodwill apparent.

Key Industry Trends

The trend in sales of retail products has been progressively more competitive, where the public will often search until they find what they believe to be the best price value available. Thrift stores can beat any regular retailer's price because all of the products are donated. Giant retailers like Wal-Mart are popular because they can sell goods at a somewhat low price. As the low bank interest rates have spurred house sales, more people have to carefully budget their incomes in order to pay their mortgages.

Industry Outlook

The industry outlook for retail sales of used consumer products is very good. There is still a lot of room in the North American market for this level of retailing.

Awareness of the incredible opportunities for fund raising for charities and for the licensees to own a prosperous Thrift Store business has never been better. Increased awareness of the global warming problem will also drive thrift sales. Re-using is one of the best ways to combat such problems, as it stops new manufacturing of the item, requires no long distant transport and saves on fuel costs and pollution.

TARGET MARKETS

Persons with limited incomes; families, environmentally aware persons, seniors and the typical "Bargain Hunter" will be the initial regular customers. These people will visit the thrift store at least weekly to see what new items have been donated – and to support the sponsoring charity.

PRICING STRATEGY

With the exception of sales events and clearances of stock that is not moving of the shelves, donated products will be priced slightly lower than direct competition. Since the prices are already so low, there is little other competition.

PROMOTION STRATEGY

_____ Thrift store plans to hold a grand opening that will be publicized with advertisements in the local paper. Posters announcing the opening of the store will be placed in high traffic areas such as community centres. Free refreshments and balloons and a draw for various sizes of gift certificates will be provided as incentives to visit the store.

STAFFING

All operations and management activities will be carried out by the owner. Volunteers from (charity) will assist.

Staffing by management with volunteers. We will do home pick ups on a certain day or days depending on the volume of requests. To start with, we will schedule all pickups on one day, then rent a small truck to collect them. As we grow, it is expected to obtain a small used cube van for collection, with the sides painted to advertise the store.

The store will be open from 10 A.M. to 6 P.M., Monday to Saturday .

Regulatory Issues

All taxes will be remitted as required in (city, State/ province). The store will comply with all local by-laws and zoning regulations. Any safety issues or building infractions discovered by Regional District inspectors will be dealt with as they arise. The store has applied for and been approved for a business license and a sales tax registration number by the relevant authorities.

Pro-Forma Balance Sheet

Current assets such as cash and inventory will continue to increase as net sales continue to increase. As the building and equipment are leased, there are no fixed assets owned by the business except for the office equipment and furniture. We will be able to pay all bills as they are due.

We see our customers as invited guests to a party, and we are the hosts. It's our job every day to make every important spect of the customer experience a little bit better.

Jeff Bezos
Amazon.com founder

HELP IS EVERYWHERE YOU LOOK!

http://www.sba.gov

The U.S. Small Business Administration (SBA) was created in 1953 as an independent agency of the federal government to aid, counsel, assist and protect the interests of small business concerns, to preserve free competitive enterprise and to maintain and strengthen the overall economy of our nation. We recognize that small business is critical to our economic recovery and strength, to building America's future, and to helping the United States compete in today's global marketplace.

Free Online Courses To Help You With Your Business

Although SBA has grown and evolved in the years since it was established in 1953, the bottom line mission remains the same. The SBA helps Americans start, build and grow businesses. Through an extensive network of field offices and partnerships with public and private organizations, SBA delivers its services to people throughout the United States, Puerto Rico, the U. S. Virgin Islands and Guam.

Another American Government Valuable Source Of Help:

http://Business.gov, click on Small Business

Free Small Business Guides On Business.gov

- Business Topics
- Start and Manage a Business
- Advertising and Marketing
- Business Law Data and Statistics
- E-Commerce
- Emergency and Disaster Planning
- Employment and HR
- Environmental Compliance
- Finance
- Franchises and Opportunities
- Government Contracting
- Import/Export
- Licenses and Permits
- Occupational Safety and Health
- Privacy and Security
- Taxes

Info On Popular Business Topics On Business.gov

- Find Small Business Grants and Loans
- Register a Business Name (DBA/Fictitious Name)
- Start a Home-Based Business

- Get Started in Government Contracting
- Learn Ten Steps to Hiring Your First Employee
- Report Unfair or Excessive Regulatory Actions

Resources For ...

- Home-Based Businesses
- Specific Industries
- Minority- Owned Businesses
- Non-Profits
- Self-Employed
- Veteran- Owned Businesses
- Woman-Owned Businesses

Canada Business Services for Entrepreneurs:
www.cbsc.org

ABOUT CANADA BUSINESS

Canada Business is a government information service for businesses and start-up entrepreneurs in Canada.

Canada Business reduces the complexity and burden of dealing with various levels of government by serving as a single point of access for federal and provincial/territorial government services, programs and regulatory requirements for business.

Services from Canada Business are available: on the web, by telephone (toll-free) and email, and in person. For specific contact information.

Telephone: 1-888-576-4444
(9:00 AM to 5:00 PM, in every time zone)
TTY: 1-800-457-8466 (for the Deaf /hard of hearing)
(8:30 AM to 6:00 PM, Eastern Time)
E-Mail: E-mail Form
Fax: 1-888-417-0442

Key Canada Business products, available free of charge from Canada Business or on the Web, include:

The Business Start-Up Assistant (BSA) is a Web site that consolidates essential information required by anyone wishing to launch a successful business..

Interactive Business Planner (IBP):

The first small business planning software designed specifically to operate on the World Wide Web. This interactive online tool will help you prepare a comprehensive business plan for your new or existing business.

Online Small Business Workshop:

A Web-based workshop that provides techniques and information for developing your business idea, starting, marketing and financing a new venture and improving an existing small business.

Info-Guides:

Brief overviews describing services and programs organized by topic (e.g., exporting, electronic commerce).

"How-to" Guides:

These guides are designed to provide an understanding of potential license, permit or registration requirements when considering the establishment of specific types of businesses in Canada.

Business Information System (BIS):

A database containing over 1 000 documents that describe business related programs, services and selected regulations of the government of Canada, the provinces and other Canada Business partners.

Fact Sheets:

These information sheets contain information about starting and maintaining a business, including product development, retail management, advertising & promotion, and market development.

Mandate and Mission

Canada Business's mandate is to serve as the primary source of up-to-date and accurate business-related information and to provide referrals on government programs, services and regulations—without charge—in all regions of Canada.

Chapter 15

About Day To Day Operations

Items for sale will vary as donations are received. These are a few of the type of articles we will be selling:

- Men's, women's & children's clothing.
- House wares
- Glassware
- Art prints and frames
- Lamps
- Sporting goods
- Kitchenware
- Electronics
- Knick-knacks
- Couches
- Tables & Chairs

These sample prices are suggestions only. Check out your competition's prices and see how they compare. You can then adjust your prices to be slightly lower than your competition's if you wish and if you are receiving donations that are in good condition and appear to be lightly used. And of course prices will depend on how high your overhead expenses are. Another way to assign prices is to compare what the item would cost new – then charge 50% or less of the new retail price for the used product. You can always lower a price, but it is difficult to raise a price once it has been seen on the floor of your store. Promoting and selling are the key ingredients to how much the market will bear, price wise.

LADIES' CLOTHING	Minimums
blouse	3.00
bathrobes	3.00
boots	2.50
coats	12.00
dresses	4.00
evening dresses	12.00
handbags	2.50

hats	1.50
jackets	5.00
suits	7.00
shoes	2.50
skirts	3.00
sweaters	3.00
slacks	3.00
jeans	6.00

MEN'S CLOTHING — Minimums

jackets	9.00
jeans	6.00
over coats	10.00
pants - shorts	2.50
raincoats	6.00
suits	8.00
slacks	3.00
shirts	2.00

sweaters	3.00
shoes	3.00
tuxedo	12.00
T-shirts	1.50
belts - ties	1.50

CHILDREN'S CLOTHING	Minimums
blouses	1.50
boots	3.00
coats	5.00
dresses	2.50
jackets	3.50
jeans	2.50
pants	3.00
shoes	2.00
skirts	1.50
sweaters	2.50

slacks	1.50
shirts	1.50

DRY GOODS	Minimums
blankets	3.00
bedspreads	3.50
curtains	2.00
drapes	7.00
pillows	2.50
sheets (each)	2.50

FURNITURE	Minimums
air conditioner	25.00
bed (double) complete	60.00
bed (single) complete	40.00
bicycles	20.00
convertible sofa (w/ mattress)	90.00
crib (w/ mattress)	25.00
carriage	20.00

chair (upholstered)	25.00
coffee table	20.00
dresser w/ mirror	35.00
desk	30.00
end table	10.00
floor lamps	10.00
high chair	15.00
kitchen table	30.00
kitchen chair	10.00
pictures and paintings	5.00
play-pens	15.00
CD player	25.00
radio	5.00
sofa	50.00
TV color (working)	50.00

MISCELLANEOUS   Minimums

broiler ovens	15.00

assorted dishes	1.00
home computer	100.00
bicycles	25.00
vacuum cleaner (working)	20.00

ITEMS NOT ACCEPTABLE AT A THRIFT STORE

- Weapons and explosives
- hazardous waste
- construction materials
- flammable products
- large appliances
- vehicle parts
- food
- mattresses (where not allowed)
- large console television

(Be aware that older style televisions, CD/dvd players, record player and other electronics may be expensive to dispose of if not sold. Especially after Christmas, you may get an influx of such electronics, as people get new ones for their home and need to dispose of the old ones. Many communities now charge a fee to dispose of these items, as there is toxic waste in them.)

After examining the article or piece of furniture, you may politely decline some items if they present safety or chemical hazards, if we are unable to repair or clean items.

Some thrift storeowners will offer to dispose of an unsaleable item for the owner, for a fee. This is just offering a service to get rid of it for them, if it can't be sold in your thrift store.

ITEMS WE GLADLY ACCEPT:

The following is a list of the items commonly sold at Thrift Stores:

Furniture Examples

Good stain and rip free furniture for any room in the house, office or patio.

Televisions, stereos, speakers, DVD and VCR players – in good working order and not too old. Bicycles, golf equipment, garden tools, table lamps, floor lamps, sports equipment, exercise equipment, skis, humidifiers

Clothing General Description

Category includes clothing, shoes, accessories, and bed and bath items.

Examples:

Clothing Men's, Woman's, Children's

Clothing Accessories, Hats, Mitts, Scarves, Ties, Nylons, Socks, Underwear

Personal Accessories Purses, Wallets, Fanny Packs, Bags

Bed and Bath Towels, Sheets, Blankets, Pillows, Curtains, Tablecloths

Shoes All types

Miscellaneous Household Goods Examples

Housewares Toys, games, puzzles, jewelry, crafts, mugs, pots, pans, candles, pictures/frames, utensils, small garden tools, china cups, vases, dishes, cutlery, stuffed animals, glassware, silverware, stemware, baskets, ornaments, hand tools

Small Electrical Toasters, radio, power tools, irons, blenders, mixers, small stereos, CD players

Books General Description

Category includes all books (hardback and paperback), magazines, records, tapes, CD's, videos, DVD's and computer software. Textbooks will often not sell.

Chapter 16

Suggested Signs

The independent operation is solely responsible for paying rent, taxes and other operating costs.

If you have any concerns you would like to raise, please contact the (charity) directly at 555-XXX-XXXX.

(or such other form as may be mutually approved by the charity and the Operator)

Any complaints concerning the store – etc. This can be painted on a 2 foot by 3 foot durable material and hung or set in the window near the entrance. It must be clear what party is operating the store. You want to handle your own problematic situations, if there are any – not the charity. Problem calls to them may cause them to discontinue your sponsorship. Some stores word it simply as: Benefiting_____ Charity

INFORMATIONAL SIGNS TO DISPLAY

Hours of Operation

Usually 10 am – 6 pm, six days a week. Check what the times the neighboring retail business are open, so you can have similar hours.

Your days off – in the beginning it will feel like you need to always be at the thrift store – and of course you do need to spend a lot of your time there, taking care of business. But do establish definite time off for yourself – otherwise you will run the risk of "burning out", if you do not maintain a balance of private time with your family and friends. Working long hours with little time off may have a way of overwhelming you if you are not watchful.

Other Signs and Displayed Items

The Thrift Stores are privately owned and operated - a licensing agreement allows the stores to mention the charities name it donates to, for a percentage of the gross store revenue.

Arrangements can be made to pick up large items (such as furniture or appliances) by phoning the store nearest you, or you can drop off used saleable goods.

How you establish your **sales policies** is important to customer satisfaction. Most thrift stores do have signs at their checkout clearly letting a purchaser know that there will be no returns, no refunds, no replacements, and no layaways. This is fair as a thrift store sells at drastically reduced prices and cannot afford to be spending time and money on such things.

Thrift store operators will find it helpful to display some of your sponsoring charity's brochures, maybe near the check out, so interested people will learn more about the charity that your store contributes to. Staff and volunteers should be aware of what activities and functions the charity provide,

Charities need to be easily understood by the public – so they will be motivated to support the store. For example animal rescue organizations, helping disadvantaged people, childcare groups, are the most common. Any good cause can be championed.

Hospitals and churches, religious groups often have thrift shops administered by a paid volunteer administrator and run by volunteers.

Chpater 17

Income Tax

Personal Income Tax

Check with your accounting professional and / or Federal Government Taxation Department for details about operating as a sole proprietor.

Rules can change annually, so you need to be current about which practices apply to your situation.

Because you will not be paid a salary or wages as an employee would be – and no deductions withheld , check with your local tax office for instructions on filing estimated tax returns.

Corporate Income Tax

If your business is operating as a corporation, you will be paid the same as an employee, with taxes deducted from your pay and submitted directly to the tax department. When the business makes a profit, it will be in the corporation's name, not to you personally. You must file a corporate income tax return, your accountant will be able to give you valuable advice about this. Usually he/she will want to discuss 'tax planning' several months in advance, so that you may be able to legally reduce the amount of tax payable.

SALES TAXES

Sales taxes are required on most items sold. The amount varies from regionally. Some areas do have lower rates on used goods, so it is best to contact your local city and state offices for information on the sales taxes for your area.

It is the business owner's responsibility to collect taxes that need to be collected. If you fail to collect the taxes, you still will be required to pay them, as well as any penalties.

Chapter 18

Final Thoughts

Positive Mental Attitude: Why Think Positively?

All of our feelings, beliefs and knowledge are derived from our thoughts, our thinking process. We are always in control of what and how we think, even when we are not aware of it. Depending on what thoughts we allow our minds to entertain, we can feel happy, sad, angry, sad or optimistic.

Thoughts are the most powerful thing that we can control. We pretty much get what we expect. The life altering difference between people is their attitudes.

The first step in changing our attitudes is to change our inner conversations.

A Positive Outlook

> *"Most folks are about as happy as they*
> *make up their minds to be"* -
>
> Abraham Lincoln

This is not to suggest that you should pretend to be happy, but that you really do have control over how positive you can be, by monitoring and choosing your thoughts.

A positive attitude is a choice you can make about how you're going to live. Key points include:

- choosing your attitude in advance – if you say to yourself on the way to work – "I choose to have a peaceful, happy day today" – that decision will actually influence your experience of the day.
- visualizing success and
- resisting negative influences

Be sure to visit our web site at

www.startthriftstore.com

for suggestions, business tips and other helpful business products that will help you in your journey towards a fulfilling and prosperous career.

Would love to hear from you as you build your business!

Sincere Regards,
Don

Printed in the United States
152234LV00002B/117/P

9 781933 817521